MODERN LABOR LAW IN THE PRIVATE AND PUBLIC SECTORS: DOCUMENTARY SUPPLEMENT
Second Edition

MODERN LABOR LAW IN THE PRIVATE AND PUBLIC SECTORS: DOCUMENTARY SUPPLEMENT

Second Edition

SETH D. HARRIS

JOSEPH E. SLATER

ANNE MARIE LOFASO

CHARLOTTE GARDEN

CAROLINA ACADEMIC PRESS

Durham, North Carolina

ISBN: 978-1-6328-4966-3

Carolina Academic Press, LLC
700 Kent Street
Durham, NC 27701
Telephone (919) 489-7486
Fax (919) 493-5668
www.caplaw.com

Printed in the United States of America
2021 Printing

(2016–Pub.3289)

Table of Contents

SHERMAN ANTITRUST ACT

Act of July 2, 1890, 26 Stat. 209, as amended; 15 U.S.C. §§ 1–7; F.C.A. 15 §§ 1–7

SEC. 1.

Every contract, combination in the form of trust or otherwise, or conspiracy, in restraint of trade or commerce among the several States, or with foreign nations, is hereby declared to be illegal. Every person who shall make any such contract or engage in any such combination or conspiracy, shall be deemed guilty of a felony, and, on conviction thereof, shall be punished by fine not exceeding one million dollars if a corporation, or, if any other person, one hundred thousand dollars, or by imprisonment not exceeding three years or by both said punishments, in the discretion of the court.

SEC. 2.

Every person who shall monopolize, or attempt to monopolize, or combine or conspire with any other person or persons, to monopolize any part of the trade or commerce among the several States, or with foreign nations, shall be deemed guilty of a felony, and, on conviction thereof, shall be punished by fine not exceeding one million dollars if a corporation, or, if any other person, one hundred thousand dollars, or by imprisonment not exceeding three years, or by both said punishments, in the discretion of the court.

SEC. 3.

Every contract, combination in form of trust or otherwise, or conspiracy, in restraint of trade or commerce in any Territory of the United States or of the District of Columbia, or in restraint of trade or commerce between any such Territory and another, or between any such Territory or Territories and any State or States or the District of Columbia, or with foreign nations or between the District of Columbia and any State or States or foreign nations, is declared illegal. Every person who shall make any such contract or engage in any such combination or conspiracy, shall be deemed guilty of a felony, and, on conviction thereof, shall be punished by fine not exceeding one million dollars if a corporation, or, if any other person, one hundred thousand dollars, or by imprisonment not exceeding three years, or by both said punishments, in the discretion of the court.

SEC. 4.

The several district courts of the United States are invested with jurisdiction to prevent and restrain violations of this act; and it shall be the duty of the several United States attorneys, in their respective districts, under the direction of the Attorney General, to institute proceedings in equity to prevent and restrain such violations. Such proceedings may be by way of petition setting forth the case and praying that such violation shall be enjoined or otherwise prohibited. When the parties complained of shall have been duly notified of such petition the court shall proceed, as soon as may be, to the hearing and determination of the case; and pending such petition and before final decree, the court may at any time make such temporary restraining order or prohibition as shall be deemed just in the premises.

SEC. 5.

Whenever it shall appear to the court before which any proceeding under section four of this act may be pending, that the ends of justice require that other parties should be brought before the court, the court may cause them to be summoned, whether they reside in the district in which the court is held or not; and subpoenas to that end may be served in any district by the marshall thereof.

SEC. 6.

Any property owned under any contract or by any combination, or pursuant to any conspiracy (and being the subject thereof) mentioned in section one of this act, and being in the course of transportation from one State to another, or to a foreign country, shall be forfeited to the United States, and may be seized and condemned by like proceedings as those provided by law for the forfeiture, seizure, and condemnation of property imported into the United States contrary to law. . . .

SEC. 7.

That the word "person" or "persons," wherever used in this act shall be deemed to include corporations and associations existing under or authorized by the laws of either the United States, the laws of any of the Territories, the laws of any State, or the laws of any foreign country.

CLAYTON ANTITRUST ACT

Act of October 15, 1914, 38 Stat. 730, as amended;
15 U.S.C. §§ 12–27; F.C.A. 15 §§ 12–27

SEC. 6. That the labor of a human being is not a commodity or article of commerce. Nothing contained in the antitrust laws shall be construed to forbid the existence and operation of labor, agricultural, or horticultural organizations, instituted for the purposes of mutual help, and not having capital stock or conducted for profit, or to forbid or restrain individual members of such organizations from lawfully carrying out the legitimate objects thereof; nor shall such organizations, or the members thereof, be held or construed to be illegal combinations or conspiracies in restraint of trade, under the anti-trust laws.

SEC. 20. That no restrain order or injunction shall be granted by any court of the United States, or a judge or the judges thereof, in any case between an employer and employees, or between employers and employees, or between employees or between persons employed and persons seeking employment, involving, or growing out of, a dispute concerning terms or conditions of employment, unless necessary to prevent irreparable injury to property, or to a property right, of the party making the application, for which injury there is no adequate remedy at law, and such property or property right must be described with particularity in the application, which must be in writing and sworn to by the applicant or by his agent or attorney.

And no such restraining order or injunction shall prohibit any person or persons, whether singly or in concert, from terminating any relation of employment, or from ceasing to perform any work or labor, or from recommending, advising or persuading others by peaceful means so to do; or from attending at any place where any such person or persons may lawfully be, for the purpose of peacefully obtaining or communicating information, or from peacefully persuading any person to work or to abstain from working; or from ceasing to patronize or to employ any party to such dispute, or from recommending, advising, or persuading others by peaceful and lawful means so to do; or from paying or giving to, or withholding from, any person engaged in such dispute, any strike benefits or other moneys or things of value; or from peaceably assembling in a lawful manner, and for lawful purposes; or from doing any act or thing which might lawfully be done in the absence of such dispute by any party thereto; nor shall any of the acts specified in this paragraph be considered or held to be violations of any law of the United States.

NORRIS-LA GUARDIA (ANTI-INJUNCTION) ACT

Act of March 23, 1932, 47 Stat. 70,
29 U.S.C. §§ 101–15; F.C.A. 29 §§ 101–15

Be it enacted by the Senate and House of Representatives of the United States of America in Congress assembled, That no court of the United States, as herein defined, shall have jurisdiction to issue any restraining order or temporary or permanent injunction in a case involving or growing out of a labor dispute, except in strict conformity with the provisions of this Act; nor shall any such restraining order or temporary or permanent injunction be issued contrary to the public policy declared in this Act.

SEC. 2. In the interpretation of this Act and in determining the jurisdiction and authority of the courts of the United States, as such jurisdiction and authority are herein defined and limited, the public policy of the United States is hereby declared as follows:

"Whereas under prevailing economic conditions, developed with the aid of governmental authority for owners of property to organize in the corporate and other forms of ownership association, the individual unorganized worker is commonly helpless to exercise actual liberty of contract and to protect his freedom of labor, and thereby to obtain acceptable terms and conditions of employment, wherefore though he should be free to decline to associate with his fellows, it is necessary that he have full freedom of association, self-organization, and designation of representatives of his own choosing, to negotiate the terms and conditions of his employment, and that he shall be free from the interference, restraint, or coercion of employees of labor, or their agents, in the designation of such representatives or in self-organization or in other concerted activities for the purpose of collective bargaining or other mutual aid or protection; therefore, the following definitions of, and limitations upon, the jurisdiction and authority of the courts of the United States are hereby enacted."

SEC. 3. Any undertaking or promise, such as is described in this section, or any other undertaking or promise in conflict with the public policy declared in section 2 of this Act, is hereby declared to be contrary to the public policy of the United States, shall not be enforceable in any court of the United States and shall not afford any basis for the granting of legal or equitable relief by any such court, including specifically the following:

Every undertaking or promise hereafter made, whether written or oral, express or implied, constituting or contained in any contract or agreement of hiring or employment between any individual, firm, company, association, or corporation, and any employee or prospective employee of the same, whereby

(a) Either party to such contract or agreement undertakes or promises not to join, become, or remain a member of any labor organization or of any employer organization; or

(b) Either party to such contract or agreement undertakes or promises that he will withdraw from an employment relation in the event that he joins, becomes, or remains a member of any labor organization or of any employer organization.

SEC. 4. No court of the United States shall have jurisdiction to issue any restraining order or temporary or permanent injunction in any case involving or growing out of any labor dispute to prohibit any person or persons participating or interested in such dispute (as these terms are herein defined), from doing, whether singly or in concert, any of the following acts:

(a) Ceasing or refusing to perform any work or to remain in any relation of employment;

(b) Becoming or remaining a member of any labor organization or of any employer organization, regardless of any such undertaking or promise as is described in section 3 of this Act;

(c) Paying or giving to, or withholding from, any person participating or interested in such labor dispute, any strike or unemployment benefits or insurance, or other moneys or things of value;

(d) By all lawful means aiding any person participating or interested in any labor dispute who is being proceeded against in, or is prosecuting, any action or suit in any court of the United States or of any state;

(e) Giving publicity to the existence of, or the facts involved in, any labor dispute, whether by advertising, speaking, patrolling, or by any other method not involving fraud or violence;

(f) Assembling peaceably to act or to organize to act in promotion of their interests in a labor dispute;

(g) Advising or notifying any person of an intention to do any of the acts heretofore specified;

(h) Agreeing with other persons to do or not to do any of the acts heretofore specified; and

(i) Advising, urging, or otherwise causing or inducing without fraud or violence the acts heretofore specified, regardless of any such undertaking or promise as is described in section 3 of this Act.

SEC. 5. No court of the United States shall have jurisdiction to issue a restraining order or temporary or permanent injunction upon the ground that any of the persons participating or interested in a labor dispute constitute or are engaged in an unlawful combination or conspiracy because of the doing in concert of the acts enumerated in section 4 of this Act.

SEC. 6. No officer or member of any association or organization, and no association or organization participating or interested in a labor dispute, shall be held responsible or liable in any court of the United States for the unlawful acts of individual officers, members, or agents, except upon clear proof of actual participation in, or actual authorization of, such acts, or of ratification of such acts after actual knowledge thereof.

SEC. 7. No court of the United States shall have jurisdiction to issue a temporary or permanent injunction in any case involving or growing out of a labor dispute, as herein defined, except after hearing the testimony of witnesses in open court (with opportunity for cross-examination), in support of the allegations of a complaint made under oath, and testimony in opposition thereto, if offered, and except after findings of fact by the court, to the effect —

(a) That unlawful acts have been threatened and will be committed unless restrained or have been committed and will be continued unless restrained, but no injunction or temporary restraining order shall be issued on account of any threat or unlawful act excepting against the person or persons, association, or organization making the threat or committing the unlawful actor actually authorizing or ratifying the same after actual knowledge thereof;

(b) That substantial and irreparable injury to complainant's property will follow;

(c) That as to each item of relief granted greater injury will be inflicted upon complainant by the denial of relief than will be inflicted upon defendants by the granting of relief;

(d) That complainant has no adequate remedy at law; and

(e) That the public officers charged with the duty to protect complainant's property are unable or unwilling to furnish adequate protection.

Such hearing shall be held after due and personal notice thereof has been given, in such manner as the court shall direct, to all known persons against whom relief is sought, and also to the chief of those public officials of the county and city within which the unlawful acts have been threatened or committed charged with the duty to protect complainant's property: Provided, however, That if a complainant shall also allege that, unless a temporary restraining order shall be issued without notice, a substantial and irreparable injury to complainant's property will be unavoidable, such a temporary restraining order may be issued upon testimony under oath, sufficient, if sustained, to justify the court in issuing a temporary injunction upon a hearing after notice. Such temporary restraining order shall be effective for no longer than five days and shall become void at the expiration of said five days. No temporary restraining order or temporary injunction shall be issued except on condition that complainant shall first file an undertaking with adequate security in an amount to be fixed by the court sufficient to recompense those enjoined for any loss, expense, or damage caused by the improvident or erroneous issuance of such order or injunction, including all reasonable costs (together with a reasonable attorney's fee), and expense of defense against the order or against the granting of any injunctive relief sought in the same proceeding and subsequently denied by the court. . . .

SEC. 8. No restraining order or injunctive relief shall be granted to any complainant who has failed to comply with any obligation imposed by law which is involved in the labor dispute in question, or who has failed to make every reasonable effort to settle such dispute either by negotiation or with the aid of any available governmental machinery of mediation or voluntary arbitration.

SEC. 9. No restraining order or temporary or permanent injunction shall be granted in a case involving or growing out of a labor dispute, except on the basis of findings of fact made and filed by the court in the record of the case prior to the issuance of such restraining order or injunction; and every restraining order or injunction granted in a case involving or growing out of a labor dispute shall include only a prohibition of such specific act or acts as may be expressly complained of in the bill of complaint or petition filed in such case and as shall be expressly included in said findings of fact made and filed by the court as provided herein.

SEC. 10. Whenever any court of the United States shall issue or deny any temporary injunction in a case involving or growing out of a labor dispute, the court shall, upon the request of any party to the proceedings and on his filing the usual bond for costs, forthwith certify as in ordinary cases the record of the case to the circuit court of appeals for its review. Upon the filing of such record in the circuit court of appeals, the appeal shall be heard and the temporary injunctive order affirmed, modified, or set aside with the greatest possible expedition, giving the proceedings precedence over all other matters except older matters of the same character. . . .

SEC. 13. When used in this Act, and for the purposes of this Act —

(a) A case shall be held to involve or to grow out of a labor dispute when the case involves persons who are engaged in the same industry, trade, craft, or occupation; or have direct or indirect interests therein; or who are employees of the same employer; or who are members of the same or an affiliated organization of employers or employees; whether such dispute is

(1) between one or more employers or associations of employers and one or more employees or associations of employees;

(2) between one or more employers or associations of employers and one or more employers or associations of employers; or

(3) between one or more employees or associations of employees and one or more employees or associations of employees; or when the case involves any conflicting or competing interests in a "labor dispute" (as hereinafter defined), of "persons participating or interested" therein (as hereinafter defined).

(b) A person or association shall be held to be a person participating or interested in a labor dispute if relief is sought against him or it, and if he or it is engaged in the same industry, trade, craft, or occupation in which such dispute occurs, or has a direct or indirect interest therein, or is a member, officer, or agent of any association composed in a whole or in part of employers or employees engaged in such industry, trade, craft, or occupation.

(c) The term "labor dispute" includes any controversy concerning terms or conditions of employment, or concerning the association or representation of persons in negotiating, fixing, maintaining, changing, or seeking to arrange terms or conditions of employment, regardless of whether or not the disputants stand in the proximate relation of employer and employee.

(d) The term "court of the United States" means any court of the United States whose jurisdiction has been or may be conferred or defined or limited by Act of Congress, including the courts of the District of Columbia.

NATIONAL LABOR RELATIONS ACT

49 Stat. 449 (1935),
as amended by Pub. L. No. 101, 80th Cong., 1st Sess., 1947,
and Pub. L. No. 257, 86th Cong., 1st Sess., 1959;
29 U.S.C. §§ 151–69, F.C.A. 29 §§ 151–69
[Title 29, Chapter 7, Subchapter II, United States Code]

FINDINGS AND POLICIES

Sec. 1. [§ 151.]

The denial by some employers of the right of employees to organize and the refusal by some employers to accept the procedure of collective bargaining lead to strikes and other forms of industrial strife or unrest, which have the intent or the necessary effect of burdening or obstructing commerce by (a) impairing the efficiency, safety, or operation of the instrumentalities of commerce; (b) occurring in the current of commerce; (c) materially affecting, restraining, or controlling the flow of raw materials or manufactured or processed goods from or into the channels of commerce, or the prices of such materials or goods in commerce; or (d) causing diminution of employment and wages in such volume as substantially to impair or disrupt the market for goods flowing from or into the channels of commerce.

The inequality of bargaining power between employees who do not possess full freedom of association or actual liberty of contract and employers who are organized in the corporate or other forms of ownership association substantially burdens and affects the flow of commerce, and tends to aggravate recurrent business depressions, by depressing wage rates and the purchasing power of wage earners in industry and by preventing the stabilization of competitive wage rates and working conditions within and between industries.

Experience has proved that protection by law of the right of employees to organize and bargain collectively safeguards commerce from injury, impairment, or interruption, and promotes the flow of commerce by removing certain recognized sources of industrial strife and unrest, by encouraging practices fundamental to the friendly adjustment of industrial disputes arising out of differences as to wages, hours, or other working conditions, and by restoring equality of bargaining power between employers and employees.

Experience has further demonstrated that certain practices by some labor organizations, their officers, and members have the intent or the necessary effect of burdening or obstructing commerce by preventing the free flow of goods in such commerce through strikes and other forms of industrial unrest or through concerted activities which impair the interest of the public in the free flow of such commerce. The elimination of such practices is a necessary condition to the assurance of the rights herein guaranteed

It is declared to be the policy of the United States to eliminate the causes of certain substantial obstructions to the free flow of commerce and to mitigate and eliminate these obstructions when they have occurred by encouraging the practice and procedure of collective bargaining and by protecting the exercise by workers of full freedom of association, self-organization, and designation of representatives of their own choosing, for the purpose of negotiating the terms and conditions of their employment or other mutual aid or protection.

DEFINITIONS

Sec. 2. [§ 152.] **When used in this Act [subchapter] —**

(1) The term "person" includes one or more individuals, labor organizations, partnerships, associations, corporations, legal representatives, trustees, trustees in cases under title 11 of the United States Code [under title 11], or receivers.

(2) The term "employer" includes any person acting as an agent of an employer, directly or indirectly, but shall not include the United States or any wholly owned Government corporation, or any Federal Reserve Bank, or any State or political subdivision thereof, or any person subject to the Railway Labor Act [45 U.S.C. § 151 et seq.], as amended from time to time, or any labor organization (other than when acting as an employer), or anyone acting in the capacity of officer or agent of such labor organization. [Pub. L. 93-360, § 1(a), July 26, 1974, 88 Stat. 395, deleted the phrase "or any corporation or association operating a hospital, if no part of the net earnings inures to the benefit of any private shareholder or individual" from the definition of "employer."]

(3) The term "employee" shall include any employee, and shall not be limited to the employees of a particular employer, unless the Act [this subchapter] explicitly states otherwise, and shall include any individual whose work has ceased as a consequence of, or in connection with, any current labor dispute or because of any unfair labor practice, and who has not obtained any other regular and substantially equivalent employment, but shall not include any individual employed as an agricultural laborer, or in the domestic service of any family or person at his home, or any individual employed by his parent or spouse, or any individual having the status of an independent contractor, or any individual employed as a supervisor, or any individual employed by an employer subject to the Railway Labor Act [45 U.S.C. § 151 et seq.], as amended from time to time, or by any other person who is not an employer as herein defined.

(4) The term "representatives" includes any individual or labor organization.

(5) The term "labor organization" means any organization of any kind, or any agency or employee representation committee or plan, in which employees participate and which exists for the purpose, in whole or in part, of dealing with employers concerning grievances, labor disputes, wages, rates of pay, hours of employment, or conditions of work.

(6) The term "commerce" means trade, traffic, commerce, transportation, or communication among the several States, or between the District of Columbia or any Territory of the United States and any State or other Territory, or between any foreign country and any State, Territory, or the District of Columbia, or within the District of Columbia or any Territory, or between points in the same State but through any other State or any Territory or the District of Columbia or any foreign country.

(7) The term "affecting commerce" means in commerce, or burdening or

obstructing commerce or the free flow of commerce, or having led or tending to lead to a labor dispute burdening or obstructing commerce or the free flow of commerce.

(8) The term "unfair labor practice" means any unfair labor practice listed in section 8 [section 158 of this title].

(9) The term "labor dispute" includes any controversy concerning terms, tenure or conditions of employment, or concerning the association or representation of persons in negotiating, fixing, maintaining, changing, or seeking to arrange terms or conditions of employment, regardless of whether the disputants stand in the proximate relation of employer and employee.

(10) The term "National Labor Relations Board" means the National Labor Relations Board provided for in section 3 of this Act [section 153 of this title].

(11) The term "supervisor" means any individual having authority, in the interest of the employer, to hire, transfer, suspend, lay off, recall, promote, discharge, assign, reward, or discipline other employees, or responsibly to direct them, or to adjust their grievances, or effectively to recommend such action, if in connection with the foregoing the exercise of such authority is not of a merely routine or clerical nature, but requires the use of independent judgment.

(12) The term "professional employee" means —

(a) any employee engaged in work (i) predominantly intellectual and varied in character as opposed to routine mental, manual, mechanical, or physical work; (ii) involving the consistent exercise of discretion and judgment in its performance; (iii) of such a character that the output produced or the result accomplished cannot be standardized in relation to a given period of time; (iv) requiring knowledge of an advanced type in a field of science or learning customarily acquired by a prolonged course of specialized intellectual instruction and study in an institution of higher learning or a hospital, as distinguished from a general academic education or from an apprenticeship or from training in the performance of routine mental, manual, or physical processes; or

(b) any employee, who (i) has completed the courses of specialized intellectual instruction and study described in clause (iv) of paragraph (a), and (ii) is performing related work under the supervision of a professional person to qualify himself to become a professional employee as defined in paragraph (a).

(13) In determining whether any person is acting as an "agent" of another person so as to make such other person responsible for his acts, the question of whether the specific acts performed were actually authorized or subsequently ratified shall not be controlling.

(14) The term "health care institution" shall include any hospital, convalescent hospital, health maintenance organization, health clinic, nursing home, extended care facility, or other institution devoted to the care of sick, infirm, or aged person.

[Pub. L. 93-360, § 1(b), July 26, 1974, 88 Stat. 395, added par. (14).]

Sec. 3. [§ 153.]

(a) [Creation, composition, appointment, and tenure; Chairman; removal of members] The National Labor Relations Board (hereinafter called the "Board") created by this Act [subchapter] prior to its amendment by the Labor Management Relations Act, 1947 [29 U.S.C. § 141 et seq.], is continued as an agency of the United States, except that the Board shall consist of five instead of three members, appointed by the President by and with the advice and consent of the Senate. Of the two additional members so provided for, one shall be appointed for a term of five years and the other for a term of two years. Their successors, and the successors of the other members, shall be appointed for terms of five years each, excepting that any individual chosen to fill a vacancy shall be appointed only for the unexpired term of the member whom he shall succeed. The President shall designate one member to serve as Chairman of the Board. Any member of the Board may be removed by the President, upon notice and hearing, for neglect of duty or malfeasance in office, but for no other cause.

(b) [Delegation of powers to members and regional directors; review and stay of actions of regional directors; quorum; seal] The Board is authorized to delegate to any group of three or more members any or all of the powers which it may itself exercise. The Board is also authorized to delegate to its regional directors its powers under section 9 [section 159 of this title] to determine the unit appropriate for the purpose of collective bargaining, to investigate and provide for hearings, and determine whether a question of representation exists, and to direct an election or take a secret ballot under subsection (c) or (e) of section 9 [section 159 of this title] and certify the results thereof, except that upon the filling of a request therefore with the Board by any interested person, the Board may review any action of a regional director delegated to him under this paragraph, but such a review shall not, unless specifically ordered by the Board, operate as a stay of any action taken by the regional director. A vacancy in the Board shall not impair the right of the remaining members to exercise all of the powers of the Board, and three members of the Board shall, at all times, constitute a quorum of the Board, except that two members shall constitute a quorum of any group designated pursuant to the first sentence hereof. The Board shall have an official seal which shall be judicially noticed.

(c) [Annual reports to Congress and the President] The Board shall at the close of each fiscal year make a report in writing to Congress and to the President summarizing significant case activities and operations for that fiscal year.

(d) [General Counsel; appointment and tenure; powers and duties; vacancy] There shall be a General Counsel of the Board who shall be appointed by the President, by and with the advice and consent of the Senate, for a term of four years. The General Counsel of the Board shall exercise general supervision over all attorneys employed by the Board (other than administrative law judges and legal assistants to Board members) and over the officers and employees in the regional offices. He shall have final authority, on behalf of the Board, in respect of the investigation of charges and issuance of complaints under section 10 [section 160 of this title], and in respect of the prosecution of such complaints before the Board, and shall have such other duties as the Board may prescribe or as may be provided by law. In case of vacancy in the office of the General Counsel the President is authorized to designate the officer or employee who shall act as General Counsel during such vacancy, but no person or persons so designated shall so act (1) for more than forty days when the Congress is in session unless a nomination to fill such vacancy shall have been submitted to the Senate, or (2) after the adjournment sine die of the session of the Senate in which such nomination was submitted.

[The title "administrative law judge" was adopted in 5 U.S.C. § 3105.]

Sec. 4. [§ 154.] [Eligibility for reappointment; officers and employees; payment of expenses]

(a) Each member of the Board and the General Counsel of the Board shall be eligible for reappointment, and shall not engage in any other business, vocation, or employment. The Board shall appoint an executive secretary, and such attorneys, examiners, and regional directors, and such other employees as it may from time to time find necessary for the proper performance of its duties. The Board may not employ any attorneys for the purpose of reviewing transcripts of hearings or preparing drafts of opinions except that any attorney employed for assignment as a legal assistant to any Board member may for such Board member review such transcripts and prepare such drafts. No administrative law judge's report shall be reviewed, either before or after its publication, by any person other than a member of the Board or his legal assistant, and no administrative law judge shall advise or consult with the Board with respect to exceptions taken to his findings, rulings, or recommendations. The Board may establish or utilize such regional, local, or other agencies, and utilize such voluntary and uncompensated services, as may from time to time be needed. Attorneys appointed under this section may, at the direction of the Board, appear for and represent the Board in any case in court. Nothing in this Act [subchapter] shall be construed to authorize the Board to appoint individuals for the purpose of conciliation or mediation, or for economic analysis. [The title "administrative law judge" was adopted in 5 U.S.C. § 3105.]

(b) All of the expenses of the Board, including all necessary traveling and subsistence expenses outside the District of Columbia incurred by the members or employees of the Board under its orders, shall be allowed and paid on the presentation of itemized vouchers therefore approved by the Board or by any individual it designates for that purpose.

Sec. 5. [§ 155.]

[Principal office, conducting inquiries throughout country; participation in decisions or inquiries conducted by member] The principal office of the Board shall be in the District of Columbia, but it may meet and exercise any or all of its powers at any other place. The Board may, by one or more of its members or by such agents or agencies as it may designate, prosecute any inquiry necessary to its functions in any part of the United States. A member who participates in such an inquiry shall not be disqualified from subsequently participating in a decision of the Board in the same case.

Sec. 6. [§ 156.] [Rules and regulations]

The Board shall have authority from time to time to make, amend, and rescind, in the manner prescribed by the Administrative Procedure Act [by subchapter II of chapter 5 of title 5], such rules and regulations as may be necessary to carry out the provisions of this Act [subchapter].

RIGHTS OF EMPLOYEES

Sec. 7. [§ 157.]

Employees shall have the right to self-organization, to form, join, or assist labor organizations, to bargain collectively through representatives of their own choosing, and to engage in other concerted activities for the purpose of collective bargaining or other mutual aid or protection, and shall also have the right to refrain from any or all such activities except to the extent that such right may be affected by an agreement requiring membership in a labor organization as a condition of employment as authorized in section 8(a)(3) [section 158(a)(3) of this title].

UNFAIR LABOR PRACTICES

Sec. 8. [§ 158.]

(a) [Unfair labor practices by employer] It shall be an unfair labor practice for an employer —

(1) to interfere with, restrain, or coerce employees in the exercise of the rights guaranteed in section 7 [section 157 of this title];

(2) to dominate or interfere with the formation or administration of any labor organization or contribute financial or other support to it: Provided, That subject to rules and regulations made and published by the Board pursuant to section 6 [section 156 of this title], an employer shall not be prohibited from permitting employees to confer with him during working hours without loss of time or pay;

(3) by discrimination in regard to hire or tenure of employment or any term or condition of employment to encourage or discourage membership in any labor organization: Provided, That nothing in this Act [subchapter], or in any other statute of the United States, shall preclude an employer from making an agreement with a labor organization (not established, maintained, or assisted by any action defined in section 8(a) of this Act [in this subsection] as an unfair labor practice) to require as a condition of employment membership therein on or after the thirtieth day following the beginning of such employment or the effective date of such agreement, whichever is the later, (i) if such labor organization is the representative of the employees as provided in section 9(a) [section 159(a) of this title], in the appropriate collective-bargaining unit covered by such agreement when made, and (ii) unless following an election held as provided in section 9(e) [section 159(e) of this title] within one year preceding the effective date of such agreement, the Board shall have certified that at least a majority of the employees eligible to vote in such election have voted to rescind the authority of such labor organization to make such an agreement: Provided further, That no employer shall justify any discrimination against an employee for non-

membership in a labor organization (A) if he has reasonable grounds for believing that such membership was not available to the employee on the same terms and conditions generally applicable to other members, or (B) if he has reasonable grounds for believing that membership was denied or terminated for reasons other than the failure of the employee to tender the periodic dues and the initiation fees uniformly required as a condition of acquiring or retaining membership;

(4) to discharge or otherwise discriminate against an employee because he has filed charges or given testimony under this Act [subchapter];

(5) to refuse to bargain collectively with the representatives of his employees, subject to the provisions of section 9(a) [section 159(a) of this title].

(b) [Unfair labor practices by labor organization]. It shall be an unfair labor practice for a labor organization or its agents —

(1) to restrain or coerce (A) employees in the exercise of the rights guaranteed in section 7 [section 157 of this title]: Provided, That this paragraph shall not impair the right of a labor organization to prescribe its own rules with respect to the acquisition or retention of membership therein; or (B) an employer in the selection of his representatives for the purposes of collective bargaining or the adjustment of grievances;

(2) to cause or attempt to cause an employer to discriminate against an employee in violation of subsection (a)(3) [of subsection (a)(3) of this section] or to discriminate against an employee with respect to whom membership in such organization has been denied or terminated on some ground other than his failure to tender the periodic dues and the initiation fees uniformly required as a condition of acquiring or retaining membership;

(3) to refuse to bargain collectively with an employer, provided it is the representative of his employees subject to the provisions of section 9(a) [section 159(a) of this title];

(4) (i)to engage in, or to induce or encourage any individual employed by any person engaged in commerce or in an industry affecting commerce to engage in, a strike or a refusal in the course of his employment to use, manufacture, process, transport, or otherwise handle or work on any goods, articles, materials, or commodities or to perform any services; or

(ii) to threaten, coerce, or restrain any person engaged in commerce or in an industry affecting commerce, where in either case an object thereof is —

(A) forcing or requiring any employer or self-employed person to join any labor or employer organization or to enter into any agreement which is prohibited by section 8(e) [subsection (e) of this section];

(B) forcing or requiring any person to cease using, selling, handling, transporting, or otherwise dealing in the products of any other producer, processor, or manufacturer, or to cease doing business with any other person, or forcing or requiring any other employer to recognize or bargain with a labor organization as the representative of his employees unless such labor organization has been certified as the representative of such employees under the provisions of section 9 [section 159 of this title]: *Provided,* That nothing contained in this clause (B) shall be construed to make unlawful, where not otherwise unlawful, any primary strike or primary picketing;

(C) forcing or requiring any employer to recognize or bargain with a particular labor organization as the representative of his employees if another labor organization has been certified as the representative of such employees under the provisions of section 9 [section 159 of this title];

(D) forcing or requiring any employer to assign particular work to employees in a particular labor organization or in a particular trade, craft, or class rather than to employees in another labor organization or in another trade, craft, or class, unless such employer is failing to conform to an order or certification of the Board determining the bargaining representative for employees performing such work:

Provided, That nothing contained in this subsection (b) [this subsection] shall be construed to make unlawful a refusal by any person to enter upon the premises of any employer (other than his own employer), if the employees of such employer are engaged in a strike ratified or approved by a representative of such employees whom such employer is required to recognize under this Act [subchapter]: Provided further, That for the purposes of this paragraph (4) only, nothing contained in such paragraph shall be construed to prohibit publicity, other than picketing, for the purpose of truthfully advising the public, including consumers and members of a labor organization, that a product or products are produced by an employer with whom the labor organization has a primary dispute and are distributed by another employer, as long as such publicity does not have an effect of inducing any individual employed by any person other than the primary employer in the course of his employment to refuse to pick up, deliver, or transport any goods, or not to perform any services, at the establishment of the employer engaged in such distribution;

(5) to require of employees covered by an agreement authorized under subsection (a)(3) [of this section] the payment, as a condition precedent to becoming a member of such organization, of a fee in an amount which the Board finds excessive or discriminatory under all the circumstances. In making such a finding, the Board shall consider, among other relevant factors, the practices and customs of labor organizations in the particular industry, and the wages currently paid to the employees affected;

(6) to cause or attempt to cause an employer to pay or deliver or agree to pay or deliver any money or other thing of value, in the nature of an exaction, for services which are not performed or not to be performed; and

(7) to picket or cause to be picketed, or threaten to picket or cause to be picketed, any employer where an object thereof is forcing or requiring an employer to recognize or bargain with a labor organization as the representative of his employees, or forcing or requiring the employees of an employer to accept

or select such labor organization as their collective-bargaining representative, unless such labor organization is currently certified as the representative of such employees:

(A) where the employer has lawfully recognized in accordance with this Act [subchapter] any other labor organization and a question concerning representation may not appropriately be raised under section 9(c) of this Act [section 159(c) of this title],

(B) where within the preceding twelve months a valid election under section 9(c) of this Act [section 159(c) of this title] has been conducted, or

(C) where such picketing has been conducted without a petition under section 9(c) [section 159(c) of this title] being filed within a reasonable period of time not to exceed thirty days from the commencement of such picketing: Provided, That when such a petition has been filed the Board shall forthwith, without regard to the provisions of section 9(c)(1) [section 159(c)(1) of this title] or the absence of a showing of a substantial interest on the part of the labor organization, direct an election in such unit as the Board finds to be appropriate and shall certify the results thereof: Provided further, That nothing in this subparagraph (C) shall be construed to prohibit any picketing or other publicity for the purpose of truthfully advising the public (including consumers) that an employer does not employ members of, or have a contract with, a labor organization, unless an effect of such picketing is to induce any individual employed by any other person in the course of his employment, not to pick up, deliver or transport any goods or not to perform any services.

Nothing in this paragraph (7) shall be construed to permit any act which would otherwise be an unfair labor practice under this section 8(b) [this subsection].

(c) [Expression of views without threat of reprisal or force or promise of benefit] The expressing of any views, argument, or opinion, or the dissemination thereof, whether in written, printed, graphic, or visual form, shall not constitute or be evidence of an unfair labor practice under any of the provisions of this Act [subchapter], if such expression contains no threat of reprisal or force or promise of benefit.

(d) [Obligation to bargain collectively] For the purposes of this section, to bargain collectively is the performance of the mutual obligation of the employer and the representative of the employees to meet at reasonable times and confer in good faith with respect to wages, hours, and other terms and conditions of employment, or the negotiation of an agreement or any question arising thereunder, and the execution of a written contract incorporating any agreement reached if requested by either party, but such obligation does not compel either party to agree to a proposal or require the making of a concession: Provided, That where there is in effect a collective-bargaining contract covering employees in an industry affecting commerce, the duty to bargain collectively shall also mean that no party to such contract shall terminate or modify such contract, unless the party desiring such termination or modification —

(1) serves a written notice upon the other party to the contract of the proposed termination or modification sixty days prior to the expiration date thereof, or in

the event such contract contains no expiration date, sixty days prior to the time it is proposed to make such termination or modification;

(2) offers to meet and confer with the other party for the purpose of negotiating a new contract or a contract containing the proposed modifications;

(3) notifies the Federal Mediation and Conciliation Service within thirty days after such notice of the existence of a dispute, and simultaneously therewith notifies any State or Territorial agency established to mediate and conciliate disputes within the State or Territory where the dispute occurred, provided no agreement has been reached by that time; and

(4) continues in full force and effect, without resorting to strike or lockout, all the terms and conditions of the existing contract for a period of sixty days after such notice is given or until the expiration date of such contract, whichever occurs later:

The duties imposed upon employers, employees, and labor organizations by paragraphs (2), (3), and (4) [paragraphs (2) to (4) of this subsection] shall become inapplicable upon an intervening certification of the Board, under which the labor organization or individual, which is a party to the contract, has been superseded as or ceased to be the representative of the employees subject to the provisions of section 9(a) [section 159(a) of this title], and the duties so imposed shall not be construed as requiring either party to discuss or agree to any modification of the terms and conditions contained in a contract for a fixed period, if such modification is to become effective before such terms and conditions can be reopened under the provisions of the contract. Any employee who engages in a strike within any notice period specified in this subsection, or who engages in any strike within the appropriate period specified in subsection (g) of this section, shall lose his status as an employee of the employer engaged in the particular labor dispute, for the purposes of sections 8, 9, and 10 of this Act [sections 158, 159, and 160 of this title], but such loss of status for such employee shall terminate if and when he is re-employed by such employer. Whenever the collective bargaining involves employees of a health care institution, the provisions of this section 8(d) [this subsection] shall be modified as follows:

(A) The notice of section 8(d)(1) [paragraph (1) of this subsection] shall be ninety days; the notice of section 8(d)(3) [paragraph (3) of this subsection] shall be sixty days; and the contract period of section 8(d)(4) [paragraph (4) of this subsection] shall be ninety days.

(B) Where the bargaining is for an initial agreement following certification or recognition, at least thirty days' notice of the existence of a dispute shall be given by the labor organization to the agencies set forth in section 8(d)(3) [in paragraph (3) of this subsection].

(C) After notice is given to the Federal Mediation and Conciliation Service under either clause (A) or (B) of this sentence, the Service shall promptly communicate with the parties and use its best efforts, by mediation and conciliation, to bring them to agreement. The parties shall participate fully and promptly in such meetings as may be undertaken by the Service for the purpose of aiding in a settlement of the dispute. [Pub. L. 93-360, July 26, 1974,

88 Stat. 395, amended the last sentence of Sec. 8(d) by striking the words "the sixty-day" and inserting the words "any notice" and by inserting before the words "shall lose" the phrase ", or who engages in any strike within the appropriate period specified in subsection (g) of this section." It also amended the end of paragraph Sec. 8(d) by adding a new sentence "Whenever the collective bargaining . . . aiding in a settlement of the dispute."]

(e) [Enforceability of contract or agreement to boycott any other employer; exception] It shall be an unfair labor practice for any labor organization and any employer to enter into any contract or agreement, express or implied, whereby such employer ceases or refrains or agrees to cease or refrain from handling, using, selling, transporting or otherwise dealing in any of the products of any other employer, or cease doing business with any other person, and any contract or agreement entered into heretofore or hereafter containing such an agreement shall be to such extent unenforceable and void: Provided, That nothing in this subsection (e) [this subsection] shall apply to an agreement between a labor organization and an employer in the construction industry relating to the contracting or subcontracting of work to be done at the site of the construction, alteration, painting, or repair of a building, structure, or other work: Provided further, That for the purposes of this subsection (e) and section 8(b)(4)(B) [this subsection and subsection (b)(4)(B) of this section] the terms "any employer," "any person engaged in commerce or an industry affecting commerce," and "any person" when used in relation to the terms "any other producer, processor, or manufacturer," "any other employer," or "any other person" shall not include persons in the relation of a jobber, manufacturer, contractor, or subcontractor working on the goods or premises of the jobber or manufacturer or performing parts of an integrated process of production in the apparel and clothing industry: Provided further, That nothing in this Act [subchapter] shall prohibit the enforcement of any agreement which is within the foregoing exception.

(f) [Agreements covering employees in the building and construction industry] It shall not be an unfair labor practice under subsections (a) and (b) of this section for an employer engaged primarily in the building and construction industry to make an agreement covering employees engaged (or who, upon their employment, will be engaged) in the building and construction industry with a labor organization of which building and construction employees are members (not established, maintained, or assisted by any action defined in section 8(a) of this Act [subsection (a) of this section] as an unfair labor practice) because (1) the majority status of such labor organization has not been established under the provisions of section 9 of this Act [section 159 of this title] prior to the making of such agreement, or (2) such agreement requires as a condition of employment, membership in such labor organization after the seventh day following the beginning of such employment or the effective date of the agreement, whichever is later, or (3) such agreement requires the employer to notify such labor organization of opportunities for employment with such employer, or gives such labor organization an opportunity to refer qualified applicants for such employment, or (4) such agreement specifies minimum training or experience qualifications for employment or provides for priority in opportunities for employment based upon length of service with such employer, in the industry or in the particular geographical area: Provided, That nothing in this subsection shall set aside the final proviso to section 8(a)(3) of this Act [subsection (a)(3) of this section]: Provided further, That any agreement which would be invalid, but for clause (1) of this subsection, shall not be a bar to a petition filed pursuant to section 9(c) or 9(e) [section 159(c) or 159(e) of this title].

(g) [Notification of intention to strike or picket at any health care institution] A labor organization before engaging in any strike, picketing, or other concerted refusal to work at any health care institution shall, not less than ten days prior to such action, notify the institution in writing and the Federal Mediation and Conciliation Service of that intention, except that in the case of bargaining for an initial agreement following certification or recognition the notice required by this subsection shall not be given until the expiration of the period specified in clause (B) of the last sentence of section 8(d) of this Act [subsection (d) of this section]. The notice shall state the date and time that such action will commence. The notice, once given, may be extended by the written agreement of both parties. [Pub. L. 93-360, July 26, 1974, 88 Stat. 396, added subsec. (g).]

REPRESENTATIVES AND ELECTIONS

Sec. 9. [§ 159.]

(a) [Exclusive representatives; employees' adjustment of grievances directly with employer] Representatives designated or selected for the purposes of collective bargaining by the majority of the employees in a unit appropriate for such purposes, shall be the exclusive representatives of all the employees in such unit for the purposes of collective bargaining in respect to rates of pay, wages, hours of employment, or other conditions of employment: Provided, That any individual employee or a group of employees shall have the right at any time to present grievances to their employer and to have such grievances adjusted, without the intervention of the bargaining representative, as long as the adjustment is not inconsistent with the terms of a collective-bargaining contract or agreement then in effect: Provided further, That the bargaining representative has been given opportunity to be present at such adjustment.

(b) [Determination of bargaining unit by Board] The Board shall decide in each case whether, in order to assure to employees the fullest freedom in exercising the rights guaranteed by this Act [subchapter], the unit appropriate for the purposes of collective bargaining shall be the employer unit, craft unit, plant unit, or subdivision thereof: Provided, That the Board shall not (1) decide that any unit is appropriate for such purposes if such unit includes both professional employees and employees who are not professional employees unless a majority of such professional employees vote for inclusion in such unit; or (2) decide that any craft unit is inappropriate for such purposes on the ground that a different unit has been established by a prior Board determination, unless a majority of the employees in the proposed craft unit votes against separate representation or (3) decide that any unit is appropriate for such purposes if it includes, together with other employees, any individual employed as a guard to enforce against employees and other persons rules to protect property of the employer or to protect the safety of persons on the employer's premises; but no labor organization shall be certified as the representative of employees in a bargaining unit of guards if such organization admits to membership, or is affiliated directly or indirectly with an organization which admits to membership, employees other than guards.

(c) [Hearings on questions affecting commerce; rules and regulations]

(1) Whenever a petition shall have been filed, in accordance with such regulations as may be prescribed by the Board —

(A) by an employee or group of employees or any individual or labor organization acting in their behalf alleging that a substantial number of employees (i) wish to be represented for collective bargaining and that their employer declines to recognize their representative as the representative defined in section 9(a) [subsection (a) of this section], or (ii) assert that the individual or labor organization, which has been certified or is being currently recognized by their employer as the bargaining representative, is no longer a representative as defined in section 9(a) [subsection (a) of this section]; or

(B) by an employer, alleging that one or more individuals or labor organizations have presented to him a claim to be recognized as the representative defined in section 9(a) [subsection (a) of this section]; the Board shall investigate such petition and if it has reasonable cause to believe that a question of representation affecting commerce exists shall provide for an appropriate hearing upon due notice. Such hearing may be conducted by an officer or employee of the regional office, who shall not make any recommendations with respect thereto. If the Board finds upon the record of such hearing that such a question of representation exists, it shall direct an election by secret ballot and shall certify the results thereof.

(2) In determining whether or not a question of representation affecting commerce exists, the same regulations and rules of decision shall apply irrespective of the identity of the persons filing the petition or the kind of relief sought and in no case shall the Board deny a labor organization a place on the ballot by reason of an order with respect to such labor organization or its predecessor not issued in conformity with section 10(c) [section 160(c) of this title].

(3) No election shall be directed in any bargaining unit or any subdivision within which, in the preceding twelve-month period, a valid election shall have been held. Employees engaged in an economic strike who are not entitled to reinstatement shall be eligible to vote under such regulations as the Board shall find are consistent with the purposes and provisions of this Act [subchapter] in any election conducted within twelve months after the commencement of the strike. In any election where none of the choices on the ballot receives a majority, a run-off shall be conducted, the ballot providing for a selection between the two choices receiving the largest and second largest number of valid votes cast in the election.

(4) Nothing in this section shall be construed to prohibit the waiving of hearings by stipulation for the purpose of a consent election in conformity with regulations and rules of decision of the Board.

(5) In determining whether a unit is appropriate for the purposes specified in subsection (b) [of this section] the extent to which the employees have organized

shall not be controlling.

(d) [Petition for enforcement or review; transcript] Whenever an order of the Board made pursuant to section 10(c) [section 160(c) of this title] is based in whole or in part upon facts certified following an investigation pursuant to subsection (c) of this section and there is a petition for the enforcement or review of such order, such certification and the record of such investigation shall be included in the transcript of the entire record required to be filed under section 10(e) or 10(f) [subsection (e) or (f) of section 160 of this title], and thereupon the decree of the court enforcing, modifying, or setting aside in whole or in part the order of the Board shall be made and entered upon the pleadings, testimony, and proceedings set forth in such transcript.

(e) [Secret ballot; limitation of elections] (1) Upon the filing with the Board, by 30 per centum or more of the employees in a bargaining unit covered by an agreement between their employer and labor organization made pursuant to section 8(a)(3) [section 158(a)(3) of this title], of a petition alleging they desire that such authorization be rescinded, the Board shall take a secret ballot of the employees in such unit and certify the results thereof to such labor organization and to the employer.

(2) No election shall be conducted pursuant to this subsection in any bargaining unit or any subdivision within which, in the preceding twelve-month period, a valid election shall have been held.

PREVENTION OF UNFAIR LABOR PRACTICES

Sec. 10. [§ 160.]

(a) [Powers of Board generally] The Board is empowered, as hereinafter provided, to prevent any person from engaging in any unfair labor practice (listed in section 8 [section 158 of this title]) affecting commerce. This power shall not be affected by any other means of adjustment or prevention that has been or may be established by agreement, law, or otherwise: Provided, That the Board is empowered by agreement with any agency of any State or Territory to cede to such agency jurisdiction over any cases in any industry (other than mining, manufacturing, communications, and transportation except where predominately local in character) even though such cases may involve labor disputes affecting commerce, unless the provision of the State or Territorial statute applicable to the determination of such cases by such agency is inconsistent with the corresponding provision of this Act [subchapter] or has received a construction inconsistent therewith.

(b) [Complaint and notice of hearing; six-month limitation; answer; court rules of evidence inapplicable] Whenever it is charged that any person has engaged in or is engaging in any such unfair labor practice, the Board, or any agent or agency designated by the Board for such purposes, shall have power to issue and cause to be served upon such person a complaint stating the charges in that respect, and containing a notice of hearing before the Board or a member thereof, or before a designated agent or agency, at a place therein fixed, not less than five days after the serving of said complaint: Provided, That no complaint shall issue based upon any unfair labor practice occurring more than six months prior to the filing of the charge with the Board and the service of a copy thereof upon the person against whom such charge is made, unless the person aggrieved thereby was prevented from filing such charge by reason of service in the armed forces, in which event the six-month period shall be computed from the day of his discharge. Any such complaint may be amended by the member, agent, or agency conducting the hearing or the Board in its discretion at any time prior to the issuance of an order based thereon. The person so complained of shall have the right to file an answer to the original or amended complaint and to appear in person or otherwise and give testimony at the place and time fixed in the complaint. In the discretion of the member, agent, or agency conducting the hearing or the Board, any other person may be allowed to intervene in the said proceeding and to present testimony. Any such proceeding shall, so far as practicable, be conducted in accordance with the rules of evidence applicable in the district courts of the United States under the rules of civil procedure for the district courts of the United States, adopted by the Supreme Court of the United States pursuant to section 2072 of title 28, United States Code [section 2072 of title 28].

(c) [Reduction of testimony to writing; findings and orders of Board] The testimony taken by such member, agent, or agency, or the Board shall be reduced to writing and filed with the Board. Thereafter, in its discretion, the Board upon notice may take further testimony or hear argument. If upon the preponderance of the testimony taken the Board shall be of the opinion that any person named in the complaint has engaged in or is engaging in any such unfair labor practice, then the Board shall state its findings of fact and shall issue and cause to be served on such person an order requiring such person to cease and desist from such unfair labor practice, and to take such affirmative action including reinstatement of employees with or without backpay, as will effectuate the policies of this Act [subchapter]: Provided, That where an order directs reinstatement of an employee, backpay may be required of the employer or labor organization, as the case may be, responsible for the discrimination suffered by him: And provided further, That in determining whether a complaint shall issue alleging a violation of section 8(a)(1) or section 8(a)(2) [subsection (a)(1) or (a)(2) of section 158 of this title], and in deciding such cases, the same regulations and rules of decision shall apply irrespective of whether or not the labor organization affected is affiliated with a labor organization national or international in scope. Such order may further require such person to make reports from time to time showing the extent to which it has complied with the order. If upon the preponderance of the testimony taken the Board shall not be of the opinion that the person named in the complaint has engaged in or is engaging in any such unfair labor practice, then the Board shall state its findings of fact and shall issue an order dismissing the said complaint. No order of the Board shall require the reinstatement of any individual as an employee who has been suspended or discharged, or the payment to him of any backpay, if such individual was suspended or discharged for cause. In case the evidence is presented before a member of the Board, or before an administrative law judge or judges thereof, such member, or such judge or judges, as the case may be, shall issue and cause to be served on the parties to the proceeding a proposed report, together with a recommended order, which shall be filed with the Board, and if no exceptions are filed within twenty days after service thereof upon such parties, or within such further period as the Board may authorize, such recommended order shall become the order of the Board and become affective as therein prescribed. [The title "administrative law judge" was adopted in 5 U.S.C. § 3105.]

(d) [Modification of findings or orders prior to filing record in court] Until the record in a case shall have been filed in a court, as hereinafter provided, the Board may at any time, upon reasonable notice and in such manner as it shall deem proper, modify or set aside, in whole or in part, any finding or order made or issued by it.

(e) [Petition to court for enforcement of order; proceedings; review of judgment] The Board shall have power to petition any court of appeals of the United States, or if all the courts of appeals to which application may be made are in vacation, any district court of the United States, within any circuit or district, respectively, wherein the unfair labor practice in question occurred or wherein such person resides or transacts business, for the enforcement of such order and for appropriate temporary relief or restraining order, and shall file in the court the record in the proceeding, as provided in section 2112 of title 28, United States Code [section 2112 of title 28]. Upon the filing of such petition, the court shall cause notice thereof to be served upon such person, and thereupon shall have jurisdiction of the proceeding and of the question determined therein, and shall have power to grant such temporary relief or restraining order as it deems just and proper, and to make and enter a decree enforcing, modifying and enforcing as so modified, or setting aside in whole or in part the order of the Board. No objection that has not been urged before the Board, its member, agent, or agency, shall be considered by the court, unless the failure or neglect to urge such objection shall be excused because of extraordinary circumstances. The findings of the Board with respect to questions of fact if supported by substantial evidence on the record considered as a whole shall be conclusive. If either party shall apply to the court for leave to adduce additional evidence and shall show to the satisfaction of the court that such additional evidence is material and that there were reasonable grounds for the failure to adduce such evidence in the hearing before the Board, its member, agent, or agency, the court may order such additional evidence to be taken before the Board, its member, agent, or agency, and to be made a part of the record. The Board may modify its findings as to the facts, or make new findings, by reason of additional evidence so taken and filed, and it shall file such modified or new findings, which findings with respect to question of fact if supported by substantial evidence on the record considered as a whole shall be conclusive, and shall file its recommendations, if any, for the modification or setting aside of its original order. Upon the filing of the record with it the jurisdiction of the court shall be exclusive and its judgment and decree shall be final, except that the same shall be subject to review by the appropriate United States court of appeals if application was made to the district court as hereinabove provided, and by the Supreme Court of the United States upon writ of certiorari or certification as provided in section 1254 of title 28.

(f) [Review of final order of Board on petition to court] Any person aggrieved by a final order of the Board granting or denying in whole or in part the relief sought may obtain a review of such order in any United States court of appeals in the circuit wherein the unfair labor practice in question was alleged to have been engaged in or wherein such person resides or transacts business, or in the United States Court of Appeals for the District of Columbia, by filing in such court a written petition praying that the order of the Board be modified or set aside. A copy of such petition shall be forthwith transmitted by the clerk of the court to the Board, and thereupon the aggrieved party shall file in the court the record in the proceeding, certified by the Board, as provided in section 2112 of title 28, United States Code [section 2112 of title 28]. Upon the filing of such petition, the court shall proceed in the same manner as in the case of an application by the Board under subsection (e) of this section, and shall have the same jurisdiction to grant to the Board such temporary relief or restraining order as it deems just and proper, and in like manner to make and enter a decree enforcing, modifying and enforcing as so modified, or setting aside in whole or in part the order of the Board; the findings of the Board with respect to questions of fact if supported by substantial evidence on the record considered as a whole shall in like manner be conclusive.

(g) [Institution of court proceedings as stay of Board's order] The commencement of proceedings under subsection (e) or (f) of this section shall not, unless specifically ordered by the court, operate as a stay of the Board's order.

(h) [Jurisdiction of courts unaffected by limitations prescribed in chapter 6 of this title] When granting appropriate temporary relief or a restraining order, or making and entering a decree enforcing, modifying and enforcing as so modified, or setting aside in whole or in part an order of the Board, as provided in this section, the jurisdiction of courts sitting in equity shall not be limited by sections 101 to 115 of title 29, United States Code [chapter 6 of this title] [known as the "Norris-LaGuardia Act"].

(i) Repealed.

(j) [Injunctions] The Board shall have power, upon issuance of a complaint as provided in subsection (b) [of this section] charging that any person has engaged in or is engaging in an unfair labor practice, to petition any United States district court, within any district wherein the unfair labor practice in question is alleged to have occurred or wherein such person resides or transacts business, for appropriate temporary relief or restraining order. Upon the filing of any such petition the court shall cause notice thereof to be served upon such person, and thereupon shall have jurisdiction to grant to the Board such temporary relief or restraining order as it deems just and proper.

(k) [Hearings on jurisdictional strikes] Whenever it is charged that any person has engaged in an unfair labor practice within the meaning of paragraph (4)(D) of section 8(b) [section 158(b) of this title], the Board is empowered and directed to hear and determine the dispute out of which such unfair labor practice shall have arisen, unless, within ten days after notice that such charge has been filed, the parties to such dispute submit to the Board satisfactory evidence that they have adjusted, or agreed upon methods for the voluntary adjustment of, the dispute. Upon compliance by the parties to the dispute with the decision of the Board or upon such voluntary adjustment of the dispute, such charge shall be dismissed.

(l) [Boycotts and strikes to force recognition of uncertified labor organizations; injunctions; notice; service of process] Whenever it is charged that any person has engaged in an unfair labor practice within the meaning of paragraph (4)(A), (B), or (C) of section 8(b) [section 158(b) of this title], or section 8(e) [section 158(e) of this title] or section 8(b)(7) [section 158(b)(7) of this title], the preliminary investigation of such charge shall be made forthwith and given priority over all other cases except cases of like character in the office where it is filed or to which it is referred. If, after such investigation, the officer or regional attorney to whom the matter may be referred has reasonable cause to believe such charge is true and that a complaint should issue, he shall, on behalf of the Board, petition any United States district court within any district where the unfair labor practice in question has occurred, is alleged to have occurred, or wherein such person resides or transacts business, for appropriate injunctive relief pending the final adjudication of the Board with respect to such matter. Upon the filing of any such petition the district court shall have jurisdiction to grant such injunctive relief or temporary restraining order as it deems just and proper, notwithstanding any other provision of law: Provided further, That no temporary restraining order shall be issued without notice unless a petition alleges that substantial and irreparable injury to the charging party will be unavoidable and such temporary restraining order shall be effective for no longer than five days and will become void at the expiration of such period: Provided further, That such officer or regional attorney shall not apply for any restraining order under section 8(b)(7) [section 158(b)(7) of this title] if a charge against the employer under section 8(a)(2) [section 158(a)(2) of this title] has been filed and after the preliminary investigation, he has reasonable cause to believe that such charge is true and that a complaint should issue. Upon filing of any such petition the courts shall cause notice thereof to be served upon any person involved in the charge and such person, including the charging party, shall be given an opportunity to appear by counsel and present any relevant testimony: Provided further, That for the purposes of this subsection district courts shall be deemed to have jurisdiction of a labor organization (1) in the district in which such organization maintains its principal office, or (2) in any district in which its duly authorized officers or agents are engaged in promoting or protecting the interests of employee members. The service of legal process upon such officer or agent shall constitute service upon the labor organization and make such organization a party to the suit. In situations where such relief is appropriate the procedure specified herein shall apply to charges with respect to section 8(b)(4)(D) [section 158(b)(4)(D) of this title].

(m) [Priority of cases] Whenever it is charged that any person has engaged in an unfair labor practice within the meaning of subsection (a)(3) or (b)(2) of section 8 [section 158 of this title], such charge shall be given priority over all other cases except cases of like character in the office where it is filed or to which it is referred and cases given priority under subsection (1) [of this section].

INVESTIGATORY POWERS

Sec. 11. [§ 161.]

For the purpose of all hearings and investigations, which, in the opinion of the Board, are necessary and proper for the exercise of the powers vested in it by section 9 and section 10 [sections 159 and 160 of this title] —

(1) [Documentary evidence; summoning witnesses and taking testimony] The Board, or its duly authorized agents or agencies, shall at all reasonable times have access to, for the purpose of examination, and the right to copy any evidence of any person being investigated or proceeded against that relates to any matter

under investigation or in question. The Board, or any member thereof, shall upon application of any party to such proceedings, forthwith issue to such party subpoenas requiring the attendance and testimony of witnesses or the production of any evidence in such proceeding or investigation requested in such application. Within five days after the service of a subpoena on any person requiring the production of any evidence in his possession or under his control, such person may petition the Board to revoke, and the Board shall revoke, such subpoena if in its opinion the evidence whose production is required does not relate to any matter under investigation, or any matter in question in such proceedings, or if in its opinion such subpoena does not describe with sufficient particularity the evidence whose production is required. Any member of the Board, or any agent or agency designated by the Board for such purposes, may administer oaths and affirmations, examine witnesses, and receive evidence. Such attendance of witnesses and the production of such evidence may be required from any place in the United States or any Territory or possession thereof, at any designated place of hearing.

(2) [Court aid in compelling production of evidence and attendance of witnesses] In case on contumacy or refusal to obey a subpoena issued to any person, any United States district court or the United States courts of any Territory or possession, within the jurisdiction of which the inquiry is carried on or within the jurisdiction of which said person guilty of contumacy or refusal to obey is found or resides or transacts business, upon application by the Board shall have jurisdiction to issue to such person an order requiring such person to appear before the Board, its member, agent, or agency, there to produce evidence if so ordered, or there to give testimony touching the matter under investigation or in question; and any failure to obey such order of the court may be punished by said court as a contempt thereof.

(3) Repealed. [Immunity of witnesses. See 18 U.S.C. § 6001 et seq.]

(4) [Process, service and return; fees of witnesses] Complaints, orders and other process and papers of the Board, its member, agent, or agency, may be served either personally or by registered or certified mail or by telegraph or by leaving a copy thereof at the principal office or place of business of the person required to be served. The verified return by the individual so serving the same setting forth the manner of such service shall be proof of the same, and the return post office receipt or telegraph receipt therefore when registered or certified and mailed or when telegraphed as aforesaid shall be proof of service of the same. Witnesses summoned before the Board, its member, agent, or agency, shall be paid the same fees and mileage that are paid witnesses in the courts of the United States, and witnesses whose depositions are taken and the persons taking the same shall severally be entitled to the same fees as are paid for like services in the courts of the United States.

(5) [Process, where served] All process of any court to which application may be made under this Act [subchapter] may be served in the judicial district wherein the defendant or other person required to be served resides or may be found.

(6) [Information and assistance from departments] The several departments

and agencies of the Government, when directed by the President, shall furnish the Board, upon its request, all records, papers, and information in their possession relating to any matter before the Board.

Sec. 12. [§ 162.]   [Offenses and penalties]

Any person who shall willfully resist, prevent, impede, or interfere with any member of the Board or any of its agents or agencies in the performance of duties pursuant to this Act [subchapter] shall be punished by a fine of not more than $5,000 or by imprisonment for not more than one year, or both.

LIMITATIONS

Sec. 13. [§ 163.]   [Right to strike preserved]

Nothing in this Act [subchapter], except as specifically provided for herein, shall be construed so as either to interfere with or impede or diminish in any way the right to strike or to affect the limitations or qualifications on that right.

Sec. 14. [§ 164.]   [Construction of provisions]

(a) [Supervisors as union members] Nothing herein shall prohibit any individual employed as a supervisor from becoming or remaining a member of a labor organization, but no employer subject to this Act [subchapter] shall be compelled to deem individuals defined herein as supervisors as employees for the purpose of any law, either national or local, relating to collective bargaining.

(b) [Agreements requiring union membership in violation of State law] Nothing in this Act [subchapter] shall be construed as authorizing the execution or application of agreements requiring membership in a labor organization as a condition of employment in any State or Territory in which such execution or application is prohibited by State or Territorial law.

(c) [Power of Board to decline jurisdiction of labor disputes; assertion of jurisdiction by State and Territorial courts] (1) The Board, in its discretion, may, by rule of decision or by published rules adopted pursuant to the Administrative Procedure Act [to subchapter II of chapter 5 of title 5], decline to assert jurisdiction over any labor dispute involving any class or category of employers, where, in the opinion of the Board, the effect of such labor dispute on commerce is not sufficiently substantial to warrant the exercise of its jurisdiction: Provided, That the Board shall not decline to assert jurisdiction over any labor dispute over which it would assert jurisdiction under the standards prevailing upon August 1, 1959. . . .

INDIVIDUALS WITH RELIGIOUS CONVICTIONS

Sec. 19. [§ 169.]

Any employee who is a member of and adheres to established and traditional tenets or teachings of a bona fide religion, body, or sect which has historically held conscientious objections to joining or financially supporting labor organizations shall not be required to join or financially support any labor organization as a condition of employment; except that such employee may be required in a contract between such employee's employer and a labor organization in lieu of periodic dues and initiation fees, to pay sums equal to such dues and initiation fees to a nonreligious, nonlabor organization charitable fund exempt from taxation under section 501(c)(3) of title 26 of the Internal Revenue Code [section 501(c)(3) of title 26], chosen by such employee from a list of at least three such funds, designated in such contract or if the contract fails to designate such funds, then to any such fund chosen by the employee. If such employee who holds conscientious objections pursuant to this section requests the labor organization to use the grievance-arbitration procedure on the employee's behalf, the labor organization is authorized to charge the employee for the reasonable cost of using such procedure. [Sec. added, Pub. L. 93-360, July 26, 1974, 88 Stat. 397, and amended, Pub. L. 96-593, Dec. 24, 1980, 94 Stat. 3452.]

LABOR MANAGEMENT RELATIONS ACT

Cited LMRA; 29 U.S.C. §§ 141–197

[Title 29, Chapter 7, United States Code]

SHORT TITLE AND DECLARATION OF POLICY

Sec. 1. [§ 141.]

(a) This Act [chapter] may be cited as the "Labor Management Relations Act, 1947." [Also known as the "Taft-Hartley Act."]

(b) Industrial strife which interferes with the normal flow of commerce and with the full production of articles and commodities for commerce, can be avoided or substantially minimized if employers, employees, and labor organizations each recognize under law one another's legitimate rights in their relations with each other, and above all recognize under law that neither party has any right in its relations with any other to engage in acts or practices which jeopardize the public health, safety, or interest.

It is the purpose and policy of this Act [chapter], in order to promote the full flow of commerce, to prescribe the legitimate rights of both employees and employers in their relations affecting commerce, to provide orderly and peaceful procedures for preventing the interference by either with the legitimate rights of the other, to protect the rights of individual employees in their relations with labor organizations whose activities affect commerce, to define and proscribe practices on the part of labor and management which affect commerce and are inimical to the general welfare, and to protect the rights of the public in connection with labor disputes affecting commerce.

TITLE I, Amendments to NATIONAL LABOR RELATIONS ACT, 29 U.S.C. §§ 151–169 (printed above)

TITLE II [Title 29, Chapter 7, Subchapter III, United States Code] CONCILIATION OF LABOR DISPUTES IN INDUSTRIES AFFECTING COMMERCE; NATIONAL EMERGENCIES

Sec. 201. [§ 171.]   [Declaration of purpose and policy]

It is the policy of the United States that —

(a) sound and stable industrial peace and the advancement of the general welfare, health, and safety of the Nation and of the best interest of employers and employees can most satisfactorily be secured by the settlement of issues between employers and employees through the processes of conference and collective bargaining between employers and the representatives of their employees;

(b) the settlement of issues between employers and employees through collective bargaining may by advanced by making available full and adequate governmental facilities for conciliation, mediation, and voluntary arbitration to aid and encourage employers and the representatives of their employees to reach

33

and maintain agreements concerning rates of pay, hours, and working conditions, and to make all reasonable efforts to settle their differences by mutual agreement reached through conferences and collective bargaining or by such methods as may be provided for in any applicable agreement for the settlement of disputes; and

(c) certain controversies which arise between parties to collective bargaining agreements may be avoided or minimized by making available full and adequate governmental facilities for furnishing assistance to employers and the representatives of their employees in formulating for inclusion within such agreements provision for adequate notice of any proposed changes in the terms of such agreements, for the final adjustment of grievances or questions regarding the application or interpretation of such agreements, and other provisions designed to prevent the subsequent arising of such controversies.

Sec. 202. [§ 172.]　[Federal Mediation and Conciliation Service]

(a) [Creation; appointment of Director] There is created an independent agency to be known as the Federal Mediation and Conciliation Service (herein referred to as the "Service," except that for sixty days after June 23, 1947, such term shall refer to the Conciliation Service of the Department of Labor). The Service shall be under the direction of a Federal Mediation and Conciliation Director (hereinafter referred to as the "Director"), who shall be appointed by the President by and with the advice and consent of the Senate. The Director shall not engage in any other business, vocation, or employment.

(b) [Appointment of officers and employees; expenditures for supplies, facilities, and services] The Director is authorized, subject to the civil service laws, to appoint such clerical and other personnel as may be necessary for the execution of the functions of the Service, and shall fix their compensation in accordance with sections 5101 to 5115 and sections 5331 to 5338 of title 5, United States Code [chapter 51 and subchapter III of chapter 53 of title 5], and may, without regard to the provisions of the civil service laws, appoint such conciliators and mediators as may be necessary to carry out the functions of the Service. The Director is authorized to make such expenditures for supplies, facilities, and services as he deems necessary. Such expenditures shall be allowed and paid upon presentation of itemized vouchers therefore approved by the Director or by any employee designated by him for that purpose.

(c) [Principal and regional offices; delegation of authority by Director; annual report to Congress] The principal office of the Service shall be in the District of Columbia, but the Director may establish regional offices convenient to localities in which labor controversies are likely to arise. The Director may by order, subject to revocation at any time, delegate any authority and discretion conferred upon him by this Act [chapter] to any regional director, or other officer or employee of the Service. The Director may establish suitable procedures for cooperation with State and local mediation agencies. The Director shall make an annual report in writing to Congress at the end of the fiscal year.

(d) [Transfer of all mediation and conciliation services to Service; effective date; pending proceedings unaffected] All mediation and conciliation functions of the

Secretary of Labor or the United States Conciliation Service under section 51 [repealed] of title 29, United States Code [this title], and all functions of the United States Conciliation Service under any other law are transferred to the Federal Mediation and Conciliation Service, together with the personnel and records of the United States Conciliation Service. Such transfer shall take effect upon the sixtieth day after June 23, 1947. Such transfer shall not affect any proceedings pending before the United States Conciliation Service or any certification, order, rule, or regulation theretofore made by it or by the Secretary of Labor. The Director and the Service shall not be subject in any way to the jurisdiction or authority of the Secretary of Labor or any official or division of the Department of Labor.

FUNCTIONS OF THE SERVICE

Sec. 203. [§ 173.]   [Functions of Service]

(a) [Settlement of disputes through conciliation and mediation] It shall be the duty of the Service, in order to prevent or minimize interruptions of the free flow of commerce growing out of labor disputes, to assist parties to labor disputes in industries affecting commerce to settle such disputes through conciliation and mediation.

(b) [Intervention on motion of Service or request of parties; avoidance of mediation of minor disputes] The Service may proffer its services in any labor dispute in any industry affecting commerce, either upon its own motion or upon the request of one or more of the parties to the dispute, whenever in its judgment such dispute threatens to cause a substantial interruption of commerce. The Director and the Service are directed to avoid attempting to mediate disputes which would have only a minor effect on interstate commerce if State or other conciliation services are available to the parties. Whenever the Service does proffer its services in any dispute, it shall be the duty of the Service promptly to put itself in communication with the parties and to use its best efforts, by mediation and conciliation, to bring them to agreement.

(c) [Settlement of disputes by other means upon failure of conciliation] If the Director is not able to bring the parties to agreement by conciliation within a reasonable time, he shall seek to induce the parties voluntarily to seek other means of settling the dispute without resort to strike, lockout, or other coercion, including submission to the employees in the bargaining unit of the employer's last offer of settlement for approval or rejection in a secret ballot. The failure or refusal of either party to agree to any procedure suggested by the Director shall not be deemed a violation of any duty or obligation imposed by this Act [chapter].

(d) [Use of conciliation and mediation services as last resort] Final adjustment by a method agreed upon by the parties is declared to be the desirable method for settlement of grievance disputes arising over the application or interpretation of an existing collective-bargaining agreement. The Service is directed to make its conciliation and mediation services available in the settlement of such grievance disputes only as a last resort and in exceptional cases.

(e) [Encouragement and support of establishment and operation of joint labor management activities conducted by committees] The Service is authorized and directed to encourage and support the establishment and operation of joint labor management activities conducted by plant, area, and industry wide committees designed to improve labor management relationships, job security and organizational effectiveness, in accordance with the provisions of section 205A [section 175a of this title]. [Pub. L. 95-524, § 6(c)(1), Oct. 27, 1978, 92 Stat. 2020, added subsec. (e).]

Sec. 204. [§ 174.]   [Co-equal obligations of employees, their representatives, and management to minimize labor disputes]

(a) In order to prevent or minimize interruptions of the free flow of commerce growing out of labor disputes, employers and employees and their representatives, in any industry affecting commerce, shall —

(1) exert every reasonable effort to make and maintain agreements concerning rates of pay, hours, and working conditions, including provision for adequate notice of any proposed change in the terms of such agreements;

(2) whenever a dispute arises over the terms or application of a collective-bargaining agreement and a conference is requested by a party or prospective party thereto, arrange promptly for such a conference to be held and endeavor in such conference to settle such dispute expeditiously; and

(3) in case such dispute is not settled by conference, participate fully and promptly in such meetings as may be undertaken by the Service under this Act [chapter] for the purpose of aiding in a settlement of the dispute.

Sec. 205. [§175.]   [National Labor-Management Panel; creation and composition; appointment, tenure, and compensation; duties]

(a) There is created a National Labor-Management Panel which shall be composed of twelve members appointed by the President, six of whom shall be elected from among persons outstanding in the field of management and six of whom shall be selected from among persons outstanding in the field of labor. Each member shall hold office for a term of three years, except that any member appointed to fill a vacancy occurring prior to the expiration of the term for which his predecessor was appointed shall be appointed for the remainder of such term, and the terms of office of the members first taking office shall expire, as designated by the President at the time of appointment, four at the end of the first year, four at the end of the second year, and four at the end of the third year after the date of appointment. Members of the panel, when serving on business of the panel, shall be paid compensation at the rate of $25 per day, and shall also be entitled to receive an allowance for actual and necessary travel and subsistence expenses while so serving away from their places of residence.

(b) It shall be the duty of the panel, at the request of the Director, to advise in the avoidance of industrial controversies and the manner in which mediation and voluntary adjustment shall be administered, particularly with reference to controversies affecting the general welfare of the country.

Sec. 205A. [§ 175a.] [Assistance to plant, area, and industry wide labor management committees]

(a) [Establishment and operation of plant, area, and industry wide committees]

(1) The Service is authorized and directed to provide assistance in the establishment and operation of plant, area and industry wide labor management committees which —

(A) have been organized jointly by employers and labor organizations representing employees in that plant, area, or industry; and

(B) are established for the purpose of improving labor management relationships, job security, organizational effectiveness, enhancing economic development or involving workers in decisions affecting their jobs including improving communication with respect to subjects of mutual interest and concern.

(2) The Service is authorized and directed to enter into contracts and to make grants, where necessary or appropriate, to fulfill its responsibilities under this section.

(b) [Restrictions on grants, contracts, or other assistance]

(1) No grant may be made, no contract may be entered into and no other assistance may be provided under the provisions of this section to a plant labor management committee unless the employees in that plant are represented by a labor organization and there is in effect at that plant a collective bargaining agreement.

(2) No grant may be made, no contract may be entered into and no other assistance may be provided under the provisions of this section to an area or industry wide labor management committee unless its participants include any labor organizations certified or recognized as the representative of the employees of an employer participating in such committee. Nothing in this clause shall prohibit participation in an area or industry wide committee by an employer whose employees are not represented by a labor organization.

(3) No grant may be made under the provisions of this section to any labor management committee which the Service finds to have as one of its purposes the discouragement of the exercise of rights contained in section 7 of the National Labor Relations Act (29 U.S.C. § 157) [section 157 of this title], or the interference with collective bargaining in any plant, or industry.

(c) [Establishment of office] The Service shall carry out the provisions of this section through an office established for that purpose.

(d) [Authorization of appropriations] There are authorized to be appropriated to carry out the provisions of this section $10,000,000 for the fiscal year 1979, and such sums as may be necessary thereafter.

[Pub. L. 95-524, § 6(c)(2), Oct. 27, 1978, 92 Stat. 2020, added Sec. 205A.]

NATIONAL EMERGENCIES

Sec. 206. [§ 176.] [Appointment of board of inquiry by President; report; contents; filing with Service]

Whenever in the opinion of the President of the United States, a threatened or actual strike or lockout affecting an entire industry or a substantial part thereof engaged in trade, commerce, transportation, transmission, or communication among the several States or with foreign nations, or engaged in the production of goods for commerce, will, if permitted to occur or to continue, imperil the national health or safety, he may appoint a board of inquiry to inquire into the issues involved in the dispute and to make a written report to him within such time as he shall prescribe. Such report shall include a statement of the facts with respect to the dispute, including each party's statement of its position but shall not contain any recommendations. The President shall file a copy of such report with the Service and shall make its contents available to the public.

Sec. 207. [§ 177.] [Board of inquiry]

(a) [Composition] A board of inquiry shall be composed of a chairman and such other members as the President shall determine, and shall have power to sit and act in any place within the United States and to conduct such hearings either in public or in private, as it may deem necessary or proper, to ascertain the facts with respect to the causes and circumstances of the dispute.

(b) [Compensation] Members of a board of inquiry shall receive compensation at the rate of $50 for each day actually spent by them in the work of the board, together with necessary travel and subsistence expenses.

(c) [Powers of discovery] For the purpose of any hearing or inquiry conducted by any board appointed under this title, the provisions of sections 49 and 50 of title 15, United States Code [sections 49 and 50 of title 15] (relating to the attendance of witnesses and the production of books, papers, and documents) are made applicable to the powers and duties of such board.

Sec. 208. [§ 178.] [Injunctions during national emergency]

(a) [Petition to district court by Attorney General on direction of President] Upon receiving a report from a board of inquiry the President may direct the Attorney General to petition any district court of the United States having jurisdiction of the parties to enjoin such strike or lockout or the continuing thereof, and if the court finds that such threatened or actual strike or lockout —

(i) affects an entire industry or a substantial part thereof engaged in trade, commerce, transportation, transmission, or communication among the several States or with foreign nations, or engaged in the production of goods for commerce; and

(ii) if permitted to occur or to continue, will imperil the national health or safety, it shall have jurisdiction to enjoin any such strike or lockout, or the continuing thereof, and to make such other orders as may be appropriate.

(b) [Inapplicability of chapter 6] In any case, the provisions of sections 101 to 115 of title 29, United States Code [chapter 6 of this title] [known as the "Norris-LaGuardia Act"] shall not be applicable.

(c) [Review of orders] The order or orders of the court shall be subject to review by the appropriate United States court of appeals and by the Supreme Court upon writ of certiorari or certification as provided in section 1254 of title 28, United States Code [section 1254 of title 28].

Sec. 209. [§ 179.]   [Injunctions during national emergency; adjustment efforts by parties during injunction period]

(a) [Assistance of Service; acceptance of Service's proposed settlement] Whenever a district court has issued an order under section 208 [section 178 of this title] enjoining acts or practices which imperil or threaten to imperil the national health or safety, it shall be the duty of the parties to the labor dispute giving rise to such order to make every effort to adjust and settle their differences, with the assistance of the Service created by this Act [chapter]. Neither party shall be under any duty to accept, in whole or in part, any proposal of settlement made by the Service.

(b) [Reconvening of board of inquiry; report by board; contents; secret ballot of employees by National Labor Relations Board; certification of results to Attorney General] Upon the issuance of such order, the President shall reconvene the board of inquiry which has previously reported with respect to the dispute. At the end of a sixty-day period (unless the dispute has been settled by that time), the board of inquiry shall report to the President the current position of the parties and the efforts which have been made for settlement, and shall include a statement by each party of its position and a statement of the employer's last offer of settlement. The President shall make such report available to the public. The National Labor Relations Board, within the succeeding fifteen days, shall take a secret ballot of the employees of each employer involved in the dispute on the question of whether they wish to accept the final offer of settlement made by their employer, as stated by him and shall certify the results thereof to the Attorney General within five days thereafter.

Sec. 210. [§ 180.]   [Discharge of injunction upon certification of results of election or settlement; report to Congress]

Upon the certification of the results of such ballot or upon a settlement being reached, whichever happens sooner, the Attorney General shall move the court to discharge the injunction, which motion shall then be granted and the injunction discharged. When such motion is granted, the President shall submit to the Congress a full and comprehensive report of the proceedings, including the findings of the board of inquiry and the ballot taken by the National Labor Relations Board, together with such recommendations as he may see fit to make for consideration and appropriate action.

COMPILATION OF COLLECTIVE-BARGAINING AGREEMENTS, ETC.

Sec. 211. [§ 181.]

(a) For the guidance and information of interested representatives of employers, employees, and the general public, the Bureau of Labor Statistics of the Department of Labor shall maintain a file of copies of all available collective bargaining agreements and other available agreements and actions thereunder settling or adjusting labor disputes. Such file shall be open to inspection under appropriate conditions prescribed by the Secretary of Labor, except that no specific information submitted in confidence shall be disclosed.

(b) The Bureau of Labor Statistics in the Department of Labor is authorized to furnish upon request of the Service, or employers, employees, or their representatives, all available data and factual information which may aid in the settlement of any labor dispute, except that no specific information submitted in confidence shall be disclosed.

EXEMPTION OF RAILWAY LABOR ACT

Sec. 212. [§ 182.]

The provisions of this title [subchapter] shall not be applicable with respect to any matter which is subject to the provisions of the Railway Labor Act [45 U.S.C. § 151 et seq.], as amended from time to time.

CONCILIATION OF LABOR DISPUTES IN THE HEALTH CARE INDUSTRY

Sec. 213. [§ 183.]

(a) [Establishment of Boards of Inquiry; membership] If, in the opinion of the Director of the Federal Mediation and Conciliation Service, a threatened or actual strike or lockout affecting a health care institution will, if permitted to occur or to continue, substantially interrupt the delivery of health care in the locality concerned, the Director may further assist in the resolution of the impasse by establishing within 30 days after the notice to the Federal Mediation and Conciliation Service under clause (A) of the last sentence of section 8(d) [section 158(d) of this title] (which is required by clause (3) of such section 8(d) [section 158(d) of this title]), or within 10 days after the notice under clause (B), an impartial Board of Inquiry to investigate the issues involved in the dispute and to make a written report thereon to the parties within fifteen (15) days after the establishment of such a Board. The written report shall contain the findings of fact together with the Board's recommendations for settling the dispute, with the objective of achieving a prompt, peaceful and just settlement of the dispute. Each such Board shall be composed of such number of individuals as the Director may deem desirable. No member appointed under this section shall have any interest or involvement in the health care institutions or the employee organizations involved in the dispute.

(b) [Compensation of members of Boards of Inquiry]

(1) Members of any board established under this section who are otherwise employed by the Federal Government shall serve without compensation but shall be reimbursed for travel, subsistence, and other necessary expenses incurred by them in carrying out its duties under this section.

(2) Members of any board established under this section who are not subject to paragraph (1) shall receive compensation at a rate prescribed by the Director but not to exceed the daily rate prescribed for GS-18 of the General Schedule under section 5332 of title 5, United States Code [section 5332 of title 5], including travel for each day they are engaged in the performance of their duties under this section and shall be entitled to reimbursement for travel, subsistence, and other necessary expenses incurred by them in carrying out their duties under this section.

(c) [Maintenance of status quo] After the establishment of a board under subsection (a) of this section and for 15 days after any such board has issued its report, no change in the status quo in effect prior to the expiration of the contract in the case of negotiations for a contract renewal, or in effect prior to the time of the impasse in the case of an initial bargaining negotiation, except by agreement, shall be made by the parties to the controversy.

(d) [Authorization of appropriations] There are authorized to be appropriated such sums as may be necessary to carry out the provisions of this section.

TITLE III [Title 29, Chapter 7, Subchapter IV, United States Code]

SUITS BY AND AGAINST LABOR ORGANIZATIONS

Sec. 301. [§ 185.]

(a) [Venue, amount, and citizenship] Suits for violation of contracts between an employer and a labor organization representing employees in an industry affecting commerce as defined in this Act [chapter], or between any such labor organization, may be brought in any district court of the United States having jurisdiction of the parties, without respect to the amount in controversy or without regard to the citizenship of the parties.

(b) [Responsibility for acts of agent; entity for purposes of suit; enforcement of money judgments] Any labor organization which represents employees in an industry affecting commerce as defined in this Act [chapter] and any employer whose activities affect commerce as defined in this Act [chapter] shall be bound by the acts of its agents. Any such labor organization may sue or be sued as an entity and in behalf of the employees whom it represents in the courts of the United States. Any money judgment against a labor organization in a district court of the United States shall be enforceable only against the organization as an entity and against its assets, and shall not be enforceable against any individual member or his assets.

(c) [Jurisdiction] For the purposes of actions and proceedings by or against labor organizations in the district courts of the United States, district courts shall be deemed to have jurisdiction of a labor organization (1) in the district in which such organization maintains its principal offices, or (2) in any district in which its duly authorized officers or agents are engaged in representing or acting for employee members.

(d) [Service of process] The service of summons, subpoena, or other legal process of any court of the United States upon an officer or agent of a labor organization, in his capacity as such, shall constitute service upon the labor organization.

(e) [Determination of question of agency] For the purposes of this section, in determining whether any person is acting as an "agent" of another person so as to make such other person responsible for his acts, the question of whether the specific acts performed were actually authorized or subsequently ratified shall not be controlling.

RESTRICTIONS ON PAYMENTS TO EMPLOYEE REPRESENTATIVES

Sec. 302. [§ 186.]

(a) [Payment or lending, etc., of money by employer or agent to employees, representatives, or labor organizations] It shall be unlawful for any employer or association of employers or any person who acts as a labor relations expert, adviser, or consultant to an employer or who acts in the interest of an employer to pay, lend, or deliver, or agree to pay, lend, or deliver, any money or other thing of value —

(1) to any representative of any of his employees who are employed in an industry affecting commerce; or

(2) to any labor organization, or any officer or employee thereof, which represents, seeks to represent, or would admit to membership, any of the employees of such employer who are employed in an industry affecting commerce;

(3) to any employee or group or committee of employees of such employer employed in an industry affecting commerce in excess of their normal compensation for the purpose of causing such employee or group or committee directly or indirectly to influence any other employees in the exercise of the right to organize and bargain collectively through representatives of their own choosing; or

(4) to any officer or employee of a labor organization engaged in an industry affecting commerce with intent to influence him in respect to any of his actions, decisions, or duties as a representative of employees or as such officer or employee of such labor organization.

(b) [Request, demand, etc., for money or other thing of value]

(1) It shall be unlawful for any person to request, demand, receive, or accept, or agree to receive or accept, any payment, loan, or delivery of any money or other thing of value prohibited by subsection (a) [of this section].

(2) It shall be unlawful for any labor organization, or for any person acting as an officer, agent, representative, or employee of such labor organization, to demand or accept from the operator of any motor vehicle (as defined in part II

of the Interstate Commerce Act [49 U.S.C. § 301 et seq.]) employed in the transportation of property in commerce, or the employer of any such operator, any money or other thing of value payable to such organization or to an officer, agent, representative or employee thereof as a fee or charge for the unloading, or in connection with the unloading, of the cargo of such vehicle: Provided, That nothing in this paragraph shall be construed to make unlawful any payment by an employer to any of his employees as compensation for their services as employees.

(c) [Exceptions] The provisions of this section shall not be applicable

(1) in respect to any money or other thing of value payable by an employer to any of his employees whose established duties include acting openly for such employer in matters of labor relations or personnel administration or to any representative of his employees, or to any officer or employee of a labor organization, who is also an employee or former employee of such employer, as compensation for, or by reason of, his service as an employee of such employer;

(2) with respect to the payment or delivery of any money or other thing of value in satisfaction of a judgment of any court or a decision or award of an arbitrator or impartial chairman or in compromise, adjustment, settlement, or release of any claim, complaint, grievance, or dispute in the absence of fraud or duress;

(3) with respect to the sale or purchase of an article or commodity at the prevailing market price in the regular course of business;

(4) with respect to money deducted from the wages of employees in payment of membership dues in a labor organization: Provided, That the employer has received from each employee, on whose account such deductions are made, a written assignment which shall not be irrevocable for a period of more than one year, or beyond the termination date of the applicable collective agreement, whichever occurs sooner;

(5) with respect to money or other thing of value paid to a trust fund established by such representative, for the sole and exclusive benefit of the employees of such employer, and their families and dependents (or of such employees, families, and dependents jointly with the employees of other employers making similar payments, and their families and dependents): Provided, That (A) such payments are held in trust for the purpose of paying, either from principal or income or both, for the benefit of employees, their families and dependents, for medical or hospital care, pensions on retirement or death of employees, compensation for injuries or illness resulting from occupational activity or insurance to provide any of the foregoing, or unemployment benefits or life insurance, disability and sickness insurance, or accident insurance; (B) the detailed basis on which such payments are to be made is specified in a written agreement with the employer, and employees and employers are equally represented in the administration of such fund, together with such neutral persons as the representatives of the employers and the representatives of employees may agree upon and in the event the employer and employee groups deadlock on the administration of such fund and there are no neutral persons empowered to break such deadlock, such agreement provides that the two groups

shall agree on an impartial umpire to decide such dispute, or in event of their failure to agree within a reasonable length of time, an impartial umpire to decide such dispute shall, on petition of either group, be appointed by the district court of the United States for the district where the trust fund has its principal office, and shall also contain provisions for an annual audit of the trust fund, a statement of the results of which shall be available for inspection by interested persons at the principal office of the trust fund and at such other places as may be designated in such written agreement; and (C) such payments as are intended to be used for the purpose of providing pensions or annuities for employees are made to a separate trust which provides that the funds held therein cannot be used for any purpose other than paying such pensions or annuities; (6) with respect to money or other thing of value paid by any employer to a trust fund established by such representative for the purpose of pooled vacation, holiday, severance or similar benefits, or defraying costs of apprenticeship or other training programs: Provided, That the requirements of clause (B) of the proviso to clause (5) of this subsection shall apply to such trust funds; (7) with respect to money or other thing of value paid by any employer to a pooled or individual trust fund established by such representative for the purpose of (A) scholarships for the benefit of employees, their families, and dependents for study at educational institutions, (B) child care centers for preschool and school age dependents of employees, or (C) financial assistance for employee housing: Provided, That no labor organization or employer shall be required to bargain on the establishment of any such trust fund, and refusal to do so shall not constitute an unfair labor practice: Provided further, That the requirements of clause (B) of the proviso to clause (5) of this subsection shall apply to such trust funds; (8) with respect to money or any other thing of value paid by any employer to a trust fund established by such representative for the purpose of defraying the costs of legal services for employees, their families, and dependents for counsel or plan of their choice: Provided, That the requirements of clause (B) of the proviso to clause (5) of this subsection shall apply to such trust funds: Provided further, That no such legal services shall be furnished: (A) to initiate any proceeding directed (i) against any such employer or its officers or agents except in workman's compensation cases, or (ii) against such labor organization, or its parent or subordinate bodies, or their officers or agents, or (iii) against any other employer or labor organization, or their officers or agents, in any matter arising under the National Labor Relations Act, or this Act [under subchapter II of this chapter or this chapter]; and (B) in any proceeding where a labor organization would be prohibited from defraying the costs of legal services by the provisions of the Labor-Management Reporting and Disclosure Act of 1959 [29 U.S.C. § 401 et seq.]; or (9) with respect to money or other things of value paid by an employer to a plant, area or industry wide labor management committee established for one or more of the purposes set forth in section 5(b) of the Labor Management Cooperation Act of 1978. [Sec. 302(c)(7) was added by Pub. L. 91-86, Oct. 14, 1969, 83 Stat. 133; Sec. 302(c)(8) by Pub. L. 93-95, Aug. 15, 1973, 87 Stat. 314; Sec. 302(c)(9) by Pub. L. 95-524, Oct. 27, 1978, 92 Stat. 2021; and Sec. 302(c)(7) was amended by Pub. L. 101-273, Apr. 18, 1990, 104 Stat. 138.]

(d) [Penalty for violations] Any person who willfully violates any of the provisions of this section shall, upon conviction thereof, be guilty of a misdemeanor and be subject to a fine of not more than $10,000 or to imprisonment for not more than one year, or both.

(e) [Jurisdiction of courts] The district courts of the United States and the United States courts of the Territories and possessions shall have jurisdiction, for cause shown, and subject to the provisions of rule 65 of the Federal Rules of Civil Procedure [section 381 (repealed) of title 28] (relating to notice to opposite party) to restrain violations of this section, without regard to the provisions of section 7 of title 15 and section 52 of title 29, United States Code [of this title] [known as the "Clayton Act"], and the provisions of sections 101 to 115 of title 29, United States Code [chapter 6 of this title] [known as the "Norris-LaGuardia Act"].

(f) [Effective date of provisions] This section shall not apply to any contract in force on June 23, 1947, until the expiration of such contract, or until July 1, 1948, whichever first occurs.

(g) [Contributions to trust funds] Compliance with the restrictions contained in subsection (c)(5)(B) [of this section] upon contributions to trust funds, otherwise lawful, shall not be applicable to contributions to such trust funds established by collective agreement prior to January 1, 1946, nor shall subsection (c)(5)(A) [of this section] be construed as prohibiting contributions to such trust funds if prior to January 1, 1947, such funds contained provisions for pooled vacation benefits.

BOYCOTTS AND OTHER UNLAWFUL COMBINATIONS

Sec. 303. [§ 187.]

(a) It shall be unlawful, for the purpose of this section only, in an industry or activity affecting commerce, for any labor organization to engage in any activity or conduct defined as an unfair labor practice in section 8(b)(4) of the National Labor Relations Act [section 158(b)(4) of this title].

(b) Whoever shall be injured in his business or property by reason of any violation of subsection (a) [of this section] may sue therefore in any district court of the United States subject to the limitation and provisions of section 301 hereof [section 185 of this title] without respect to the amount in controversy, or in any other court having jurisdiction of the parties, and shall recover the damages by him sustained and the cost of the suit. . . .

TITLE V[Title 29, Chapter 7, Subchapter I, United States Code]

DEFINITIONS

Sec. 501. [§ 142.]   When used in this Act [chapter] —

(1) The term "industry affecting commerce" means any industry or activity in commerce or in which a labor dispute would burden or obstruct commerce or tend to burden or obstruct commerce or the free flow of commerce.

(2) The term "strike" includes any strike or other concerted stoppage of work by employees (including a stoppage by reason of the expiration of a collective-bargaining agreement) and any concerted slowdown or other concerted interruption of operations by employees.

(3) The terms "commerce," "labor disputes," "employer," "employee," "labor organization," "representative," "person," and "supervisor" shall have the same meaning as when used in the National Labor Relations Act as amended by this Act [in subchapter II of this chapter].

SAVING PROVISION

Sec. 502. [§ 143.]   [Abnormally dangerous conditions]

Nothing in this Act [chapter] shall be construed to require an individual employee to render labor or service without his consent, nor shall anything in this Act [chapter] be construed to make the quitting of his labor by an individual employee an illegal act; nor shall any court issue any process to compel the performance by an individual employee of such labor or service, without his consent; nor shall the quitting of labor by an employee or employees in good faith because of abnormally dangerous conditions for work at the place of employment of such employee or employees be deemed a strike under this Act [chapter].

LABOR-MANAGEMENT REPORTING AND DISCLOSURE ACT[1]

Pub. L. No. 86-257, 86th Cong., 2d Sess., 1959,
73 Stat. 519, as amended;
29 U.S.C. §§ 401–531; F.C.A. 29 §§ 401–531 [Selected provisions]

SHORT TITLE

SEC. 1. This Act may be cited as the "Labor-Management Reporting and Disclosure Act of 1959."

DECLARATION OF FINDINGS, PURPOSES, AND POLICY

SEC. 2.

(a) The Congress finds that, in the public interest, it continues to be the responsibility of the Federal Government to protect employees' rights to organize, choose their own representatives, bargain collectively, and otherwise engage in concerted activities for their mutual aid or protection; that the relations between employers and labor organizations and the millions of workers they represent have a substantial impact on the commerce of the Nation; and that in order to accomplish the objective of a free flow of commerce it is essential that labor organizations, employers, and their officials adhere to the highest standards of responsibility and ethical conduct in administering the affairs of their organizations, particularly as they affect labor-management relations.

(b) The Congress further finds, from recent investigations in the labor and management fields, that there have been a number of instances of breach of trust, corruption, disregard of the rights of individual employees, and other failures to observe high standards of responsibility and ethical conduct which require further and supplementary legislation that will afford necessary protection of the rights and interests of employees and the public generally as they relate to the activities of labor organizations, employers, labor relations consultants, and their officers and representatives.

(c) The Congress, therefore, further finds and declares that the enactment of this Act is necessary to eliminate or prevent improper practices on the part of labor organizations, employers, labor relations consultants, and their officers and representatives which distort and defeat the policies of the Labor Management Relations Act, 1947, as amended, and the Railway Labor Act, as amended, and have the tendency or necessary effect of burdening or obstructing commerce by (1) impairing the efficiency, safety, or operation of the instrumentalities of commerce; (2) occurring in the current of commerce; (3) materially affecting, restraining, or controlling the flow of raw materials or manufactured or processed goods into or from the channels of commerce, or the prices of such materials or goods in

---

[1] Title VII, § 201(d) and (e), and § 505 of the LMRDA amend the National Labor Relations Act and the Labor Management Relations Act. These provisions are incorporated in the appropriate sections of those statutes, and are omitted here.

commerce; or (4) causing diminution of employment and wages in such volume as substantially to impair or disrupt the market for goods flowing into or from the channels of commerce.

DEFINITIONS

SEC. 3. For the purposes of title I, II, III, IV, V (except section 505), and VI of this Act —

. . . .

(h) "Trusteeship" means any receivership, trusteeship, or other method of supervision or control whereby a labor organization suspends the autonomy otherwise available to a subordinate body under its constitution or bylaws. . . .

(k) "Secret ballot" means the expression by ballot, voting machine, or otherwise, but in no event by proxy, of a choice with respect to any election or vote taken upon any matter, which is cast in such a manner that the person expressing such choice cannot be identified with the choice expressed. . . .

(m) "Labor relations consultant" means any person who, for compensation, advises or represents an employer, employer organization, or labor organization concerning employee organizing, concerted activities, or collective bargaining activities.

(n) "Officer" means any constitutional officer, any person authorized to perform the functions of president, vice president, secretary, treasurer, or other executive functions of a labor organization, and any member of its executive board or similar governing body.

(o) "Member" or "member in good standing", when used in reference to a labor organization, includes any person who has fulfilled the requirements for membership in such organization, and who neither has voluntarily withdrawn from membership nor has been expelled or suspended from membership after appropriate proceedings consistent with lawful provisions of the constitution and bylaws of such organization.

TITLE I
BILL OF RIGHTS OF MEMBERS OF LABOR ORGANIZATIONS

BILL OF RIGHTS

SEC. 101.

(a)

(1) EQUAL RIGHTS. — Every member of a labor organization shall have equal rights and privileges within such organization to nominate candidates, to vote in elections or referendums of the labor organization, to attend membership meetings, and to participate in the deliberations and voting upon the business of such meetings, subject to reasonable rules and regulations in such organization's constitution and bylaws.

(2) FREEDOM OF SPEECH AND ASSEMBLY. — Every member of any labor organization shall have the right to meet and assemble freely with other members; and to express any views, arguments or opinions; and to express at meetings of the labor organization his views, upon candidates in an election of the labor organization or upon any business properly before the meeting, subject to the organization's established and reasonable rules pertaining to the conduct of meetings: Provided, That nothing herein shall be construed to impair the right of a labor organization to adopt and enforce reasonable rules as to the responsibility of every member toward the organization as an institution and to his refraining from conduct that would interfere with its performance of its legal or contractual obligations.

(3) DUES, INITIATION FEES, AND ASSESSMENTS. — Except in the case of a federation of national or international labor organizations, the rates of dues and initiation fees payable by members of any labor organization in effect on the date of enactment of this Act shall not be increased, and no general or special assessment shall be levied upon such members, except —

(A) in the case of a local labor organization, (i) by majority vote by secret ballot of the members in good standing voting at a general or special membership meeting, after reasonable notice of the intention to vote upon such question, or (ii) by majority vote of the members in good standing voting in a membership referendum conducted by secret ballot; or

(B) in the case of a labor organization, other than a local labor organization or a federation of national or international labor organizations, (i) by majority vote of the delegates voting at a regular convention, or at a special convention of such labor organization held upon not less than thirty days' written notice to the principal office of each local or constituent labor organization entitled to such notice, or (ii) by majority vote of the members in good standing of such labor organization voting in a membership referendum conducted by secret ballot, or (iii) by majority vote of the members of the executive board or similar governing body of such labor organization, pursuant to express authority contained in the constitution and bylaws of such labor organization, pursuant to express authority contained in the constitution and bylaws of such labor organization: Provided, That such action on the part of the executive board or similar governing body shall be effective only until the next regular convention of such labor organization.

(4) PROTECTION OF THE RIGHT TO SUE. — No labor organization shall limit the right of any member thereof to institute an action in any court, or in a proceeding before any administrative agency, irrespective of whether or not the labor organization or its officers are named as defendants or respondents in such action or proceeding, or the right of any member of a labor organization to appear as a witness in any judicial, administrative, or legislative proceeding, or to petition any legislature or to communicate with any legislator: Provided, That any such member may be required to exhaust reasonable hearing procedures (but not to exceed a four-month lapse of time) within such organization, before instituting legal or administrative proceedings against such organizations or any officer thereof: And provided further, That no interested employer or employer

association shall directly or indirectly finance, encourage, or participate in, except as a party, any such action, proceeding, appearance, or petition.

(5) SAFEGUARDS AGAINST IMPROPER DISCIPLINARY ACTION. — No member of any labor organization may be fined, suspended, expelled, or otherwise disciplined except for nonpayment of dues by such organization or by any officer thereof unless such member has been (A) served with written specific charges; (B) given a reasonable time to prepare his defense; (C) afforded a full and fair hearing.

(b) Any provision of the constitution and bylaws of any labor organization which is inconsistent with the provisions of this section shall be of no force or effect.

CIVIL ENFORCEMENT

SEC. 102. Any person whose rights secured by the provisions of this title have been infringed by any violation of this title may bring a civil action in a district court of the United States for such relief (including injunctions) as may be appropriate. Any such action against a labor organization shall be brought in the district court of the United States for the district where the alleged violation occurred, or where the principal office of such labor organization is located. . . .

RIGHT TO COPIES OF COLLECTIVE BARGAINING AGREEMENTS

SEC. 104. It shall be the duty of the secretary or corresponding principal officer of each labor organization, in the case of a local labor organization, to forward a copy of each collective bargaining agreement made by such labor organization with any employer to any employee who requests such a copy and whose rights as such employee are directly affected by such agreement, and in the case of a labor organization other than a local labor organization, to forward a copy of any such agreement to each constituent unit which has members directly affected by such agreement; and such officer shall maintain at the principal office of the labor organization of which he is an officer copies of any such agreement made or received by such labor organization, which copies shall be available for inspection by any member or by any employee whose rights are affected by such agreement. The provisions of section 210 shall be applicable in the enforcement of this section.

INFORMATION AS TO ACT

SEC. 105. Every labor organization shall inform its members concerning the provisions of this Act.

TITLE II
REPORTING BY LABOR ORGANIZATIONS, OFFICERS AND EMPLOYEES OF LABOR ORGANIZATIONS, AND EMPLOYERS
REPORT OF LABOR ORGANIZATIONS

SEC. 201.

(a) Every labor organization shall adopt a constitution and bylaws and shall file a copy thereof with the Secretary, together with a report, signed by its president and secretary or corresponding principal officers, containing the following information —

(1) the name of the labor organization, its mailing address, and any other address at which it maintains its principal office or at which it keeps the records referred to in this title;

(2) the name and title of each of its officers;

(3) the initiation fee or fees required from a new or transferred member and fees for work permits required by the reporting labor organization;

(4) the regular dues or fees or other periodic payments required to remain a member of the reporting labor organization; and

(5) detailed statements, or references to specific provisions of documents filed under this subsection which contain such statements, showing the provision made and procedures followed with respect to each of the following: (A) qualifications for or restrictions on membership, (B) levying of assessments, (C) participation in insurance or other benefit plans, (D) authorization for disbursement of funds of the labor organization, (E) audit of financial transactions of the labor organization, (F) the calling of regular and special meetings, (G) the selection of officers and stewards and of any representatives to other bodies composed of labor organizations' representatives, with a specific statement of the manner in which each officer was elected, appointed, or otherwise selected, (H) discipline or removal of officers or agents for breaches of their trust, (I) imposition of fines, suspensions, and expulsions of members, including the grounds for such action and any provision made for notice, hearing, judgment on the evidence, and appeal procedures, (J) authorization for bargaining demands, (K) ratification of contract terms, (L) authorization for strikes, and (M) issuance of work permits. Any change in the information required by this subsection shall be reported to the Secretary at the time the reporting labor organization files with the Secretary the annual financial report required by subsection (b).

(b) Every labor organization shall file annually with the Secretary a financial report signed by its president and treasurer or corresponding principal officers containing the following information in such detail as may be necessary accurately to disclose its financial condition and operations for its preceding fiscal year (1) assets and liabilities at the beginning and end of the fiscal year; (2) receipts of any kind and the sources thereof; (3) salary, allowances, and other direct or indirect disbursements (including reimbursed expenses) to each officer and also to each employee who, during such fiscal year, received more than $10,000 in the aggregate from such labor organization and any other labor organization affiliated with it or with which it is affiliated, or which is affiliated with the same national or international labor organization; (4) direct and indirect loans made to any officer, employee, or member, which aggregated more than $250 during the fiscal year, together with a statement of the purpose, security, if any, and arrangements for repayment; (5) direct and indirect loans to any business enterprise, together with a statement of the purpose, security, if any, and arrangements for repayment; and (6) other disbursements made by it including the purposes thereof; all in such categories as the Secretary may prescribe.

(c) Every labor organization required to submit a report under this title shall make available the information required to be contained in such report to all of its members, and every such labor organization and its officers shall be under a duty enforceable at the suit of any member of such organization in any State court of competent jurisdiction or in the district court of the United States for the district in which such labor organization maintains its principal office, to permit such member for just cause to examine any books, records, and accounts necessary to verify such report. The court in such action may, in its discretion, in addition to any judgment awarded to the plaintiff or plaintiffs, allow a reasonable attorney's fee to be paid by the defendant, and costs of the action. . . .

REPORT OF EMPLOYERS

SEC. 203.

(a) Every employer who in any fiscal year made —

(1) any payment or loan, direct or indirect, of money or other thing of value (including reimbursed expenses), or any promise or agreement therefor, to any labor organization or officer, agent, shop steward, or other representative of a labor organization, or employee of any labor organization, except (A) payments or loans made by any national or State bank, credit union, insurance company, savings and loan association or other credit institution and (B) payments of the kind referred to in section 302(c) of the Labor Management Relations Act, 1947, as amended:

(2) any payment (including reimbursed expenses) to any of his employees, or any group or committee of such employees, for the purpose of causing such employee or group or committee of employees to persuade other employees to exercise or not to exercise, or as the manner of exercising, the right to organize and bargain collectively through representatives of their own choosing unless such payments were contemporaneously or previously disclosed to such other employees;

(3) any expenditure, during the fiscal year, where an object thereof, directly or indirectly, is to interfere with, restrain, or coerce employees in the exercise of the right to organize and bargain collectively through representatives of their own choosing, or is to obtain information concerning the activities of employees or a labor organization in connection with a labor dispute involving such employer, except for use solely in conjunction with an administrative or arbitral proceeding or a criminal or civil judicial proceeding;

(4) any agreement or arrangement with a labor relations consultant or other independent contractor or organization pursuant to which such person undertakes activities where an object thereof, directly or indirectly, is to persuade employees to exercise or not to exercise, or persuade employees as to the manner of exercising, the right to organize and bargain collectively through representatives of their own choosing, or undertakes to supply such employer with information concerning the activities of employees or a labor organization in connection with a labor dispute involving such employer, except information for use solely in conjunction with an administrative or arbitral proceeding or a criminal or civil judicial proceeding; or

(5) any payment (including reimbursed expenses) pursuant to an agreement or arrangement described in subdivision (4); shall file with the Secretary a report, in a form prescribed by him, signed by its president and treasurer or corresponding principal officers showing in detail the date and amount of each such payment, loan, promise, agreement, or arrangement and the name, address, and position, if any, in any firm or labor organization of the person to whom it was made and a full explanation of the circumstances of all such payments, including the terms of any agreement or understanding pursuant to which they were made.

(b) Every person who pursuant to any agreement or arrangement with an employer undertakes activities where an object thereof is, directly or indirectly —

(1) to persuade employees to exercise or not to exercise, or persuade employees as to the manner of exercising, the right to organize and bargain collectively through representatives of their own choosing; or

(2) to supply an employer with information concerning the activities of employees or a labor organization in connection with a labor dispute involving such employer, except information for use solely in conjunction with an administrative or arbitral proceeding or a criminal or civil judicial proceeding; shall file within thirty days after entering into such agreement or arrangement a report with the Secretary, signed by its president and treasurer or corresponding principal officers, containing the name under which such person is engaged in doing business and the address of its principal office, and a detailed statement of the terms and conditions of such agreement or arrangement. Every such person shall file annually, with respect to each fiscal year during which payments were made as a result of such an agreement or arrangement, a report with the Secretary, signed by its president and treasurer or corresponding principal officers, containing a statement (A) of its receipts of any kind from employers on account of labor relations advice or services, designating the sources thereof, and (B) of its disbursements of any kind, in connection with such services and the purposes thereof. In each such case such information shall be set forth in such categories as the Secretary may prescribe.

(c) Nothing in this section shall be construed to require any employer or other person to file a report covering the services of such person by reason of his giving or agreeing to give advice to such employer or representing or agreeing to represent such employer before any court, administrative agency, or tribunal of arbitration or engaging or agreeing to engage in collective bargaining on behalf of such employer with respect to wages, hours, or other terms or conditions of employment or the negotiation of an agreement or any question arising thereunder.

(d) Nothing contained in this section shall be construed to require an employer to file a report under subsection (a) unless he has made an expenditure, payment, loan, agreement, or arrangement of the kind described therein. Nothing contained in this section shall be construed to require any other person to file a report under subsection (b) unless he was a party to an agreement or arrangement of the kind described therein.

(e) Nothing contained in this section shall be construed to require any regular officer, supervisor, or employee of an employer to file a report in connection with services rendered to such employer nor shall any employer be required to file a report covering expenditures made to any regular officer, supervisor, or employee of an employer as compensation for service as a regular officer, supervisor, or employee of such employer.

(f) Nothing contained in this section shall be construed as an amendment to, or modification of the rights protected by, section 8(c) of the National Labor Relations Act, as amended. . . .

ATTORNEY-CLIENT COMMUNICATIONS EXEMPTED

SEC. 204. Nothing contained in this Act shall be construed to require an attorney who is a member in good standing of the bar of any State, to include in any report required to be filed pursuant to the provisions of this Act any information which was lawfully communicated to such attorney by any of his clients in the course of a legitimate attorney-client relationship.

REPORTS MADE PUBLIC INFORMATION

SEC. 205.

(a) The contents of the reports and documents filed with the Secretary pursuant to sections 201, 202, 203, and 211 shall be public information, and the Secretary may publish any information and data which he obtains pursuant to the provisions of this title. The Secretary may use the information and data for statistical and research purposes, and compile and publish such studies, analyses, reports, and surveys based thereon as he may deem appropriate. . . .

(b) The Secretary shall by regulation make reasonable provision for the inspection and examination, on the request of any person, of the information and data contained in any report or other document filed with him pursuant to sections 201, 202, 203, or 211.

(c) The Secretary shall by regulation provide for the furnishing by the Department of Labor of copies of reports or other documents filed with the Secretary pursuant to this title, upon payment of a charge based upon the cost of the service. . . .

CRIMINAL PROVISIONS

SEC. 209.

(a) Any person who willfully violates this title shall be fined not more than $10,000 or imprisoned for not more than one year, or both.

(b) Any person who makes a false statement or representation of a material fact, knowing it to be false, or who knowingly fails to disclose a material fact, in any document, report, or other information required under the provisions of this title shall be fined not more than 10,000 or imprisoned for not more than one year, or both.

(c) Any person who willfully makes a false entry in or willfully conceals, withholds, or destroys any books, records, reports, or statements required to be kept by any provision of this title shall be fined not more than $10,000 or imprisoned for not more than one year, or both. (d) Each individual required to sign reports under sections 201 and 203 shall be personally responsible for the filing of such reports and for any statement contained therein which he knows to be false.

CIVIL ENFORCEMENT

SEC. 210. Whenever it shall appear that any person has violated or is about to violate any of the provisions of this title, the Secretary may bring a civil action for such relief (including injunctions) as may be appropriate. Any such action may be brought in the district court of the United States where the violation occurred or, at the option of the parties, in the United States District Court for the District of Columbia. . . .

TITLE III
TRUSTEESHIPS

REPORTS

SEC. 301.

(a) Every labor organization which has or assumes trusteeship over any subordinate labor organization shall file with the Secretary within thirty days after the date of the enactment of this Act or the imposition of any such trusteeship, and semiannually thereafter, a report, signed by its president and treasurer or corresponding principal officers, as well as by the trustees of such subordinate labor organization, containing the following information: (1) the name and address of the subordinate organization; (2) the date of establishing the trusteeship; (3) a detailed statement of the reason or reasons for establishing or continuing the trusteeship; and (4) the nature and extent of participation by the membership of the subordinate organization in the selection of delegates to represent such organization in regular or special conventions or other policy-determining bodies and in the election of officers of the labor organization which has assumed trusteeship over such subordinate organization. The initial report shall also include a full and complete account of the financial condition of such subordinate organization as of the time trusteeship was assumed over it. During the continuance of a trusteeship the labor organization which has assumed trusteeship over a subordinate labor organization shall file on behalf of the subordinate labor organization the annual financial report required by section 201(b) signed by the president and treasurer or corresponding principal officers of the labor organization which has assumed such trusteeship and the trustees of the subordinate labor organization.

(b) The provisions of sections 201(c), 205, 206, 208, and 210 shall be applicable to reports filed under this title.

(c) Any person who willfully violates this section shall be fined not more than $10,000 or imprisoned for not more than one year, or both.

(d) Any person who makes a false statement or representation of a material fact, knowing it to be false, or who knowingly fails to disclose a material fact, in any report required under the provisions of this section or willfully makes any false entry in or willfully withholds, conceals, or destroys any documents, books, records, reports, or statements upon which such report is based, shall be fined not more than $10,000 or imprisoned for not more than one year, or both. . . .

PURPOSES FOR WHICH A TRUSTEESHIP MAY BE ESTABLISHED

SEC. 302. Trusteeships shall be established and administered by a labor organization over a subordinate body only in accordance with the constitution and bylaws of the organization which has assumed trusteeship over the subordinate body and for the purpose of correcting corruption or financial malpractice, assuring the performance of collective bargaining agreements or other duties of a bargaining representative, restoring democratic procedures, or otherwise carrying out the legitimate objects of such labor organization.

UNLAWFUL ACTS RELATING TO LABOR ORGANIZATION UNDER TRUSTEESHIP

SEC. 303.

(a) During any period when a subordinate body of a labor organization is in trusteeship, it shall be unlawful (1) to count the vote of delegates from such body in any convention or election of officers of the labor organization unless the delegates have been chosen by secret ballot in an election in which all the members in good standing of such subordinate body were eligible to participate, or (2) to transfer to such organization any current receipts or other funds of the subordinate body except the normal per capita tax and assessments payable by subordinate bodies not in trusteeship: Provided, That nothing herein contained shall prevent the distribution of the assets of a labor organization in accordance with its constitution and bylaws upon the bona fide dissolution thereof.

(b) Any person who willfully violates this section shall be fined not more than $10,000 or imprisoned for not more than one year, or both.

ENFORCEMENT

SEC. 304.

(a) Upon the written complaint of any member or subordinate body of a labor organization alleging that such organization has violated the provisions of this title (except section 301) the Secretary shall investigate the complaint and if the Secretary finds probable cause to believe that such violation has occurred and has not been remedied he shall, without disclosing the identity of the complainant, bring a civil action in any district court of the United States having jurisdiction of the labor organization for such relief (including injunctions) as may be appropriate. Any member or subordinate body of a labor organization affected by any violation of this title (except section 301) may bring a civil action in any district court of the United States having jurisdiction of the labor organization for such relief (including injunctions) as may be appropriate. . . .

(c) In any proceeding pursuant to this section a trusteeship established by a labor organization in conformity with the procedural requirements of its constitution and bylaws and authorized or ratified after a fair hearing either before the executive board or before such other body as may be provided in accordance with its constitution or bylaws shall be presumed valid for a period of eighteen months from the date of its establishment and shall not be subject to attack during such period except upon clear and convincing proof that the trusteeship was not established or maintained in good faith for a purpose allowable under section 302. After the expiration of eighteen months the trusteeship shall be presumed invalid in any such proceeding and its discontinuance shall be decreed unless the labor organization shall show by clear and convincing proof that the continuation of the trusteeship is necessary for a purpose allowable under section 302. In the latter event the court may dismiss the complaint or retain jurisdiction of the cause on such conditions and for such period as it deems appropriate. . . .

TITLE IV
ELECTIONS

TERMS OF OFFICE; ELECTION PROCEDURES

SEC. 401.

(a) Every national or international labor organization, except a federation of national or international labor organizations, shall elect its officers not less often than once every five years either by secret ballot among the members in good standing or at a convention of delegates chosen by secret ballot.

(b) Every local labor organization shall elect its officers not less often than once every three years by secret ballot among the members in good standing.

(c) Every national or international labor organization, except a federation of national or international labor organizations, and every local labor organization, and its officers, shall be under a duty, enforceable at the suit of any bona fide candidate for office in such labor organization in the district court of the United States in which such labor organization maintains its principal office, to comply with all reasonable requests of any candidate to distribute by mail or otherwise at the candidate's expense campaign literature in aid of such person's candidacy to all members in good standing of such labor organization and to refrain from discrimination in favor of or against any candidate with respect to the use of lists of members, and whenever such labor organizations or its officers authorize the distribution by mail or otherwise to members of campaign literature on behalf of any candidate or of the labor organization itself with reference to such election, similar distribution at the request of any other bona fide candidate shall be made by such labor organization and its officers, with equal treatment as to the expense of such distribution. Every bona fide candidate shall have the right, once within 30 days prior to an election of a labor organization in which he is a candidate, to inspect a list containing the names and last known addresses of all members of the labor organization who are subject to a collective bargaining agreement requiring membership therein as a condition of employment, which list shall be maintained and kept at the principal office of such labor organization by a designated official thereof. Adequate safeguards to insure a fair election shall be provided, including the right of any candidate to have an observer at the polls and at the counting of the ballots.

(d) Officers of intermediate bodies, such as general committees, system boards, joint boards, or joint councils, shall be elected not less often than once every four years by secret ballot among the members in good standing or by labor organization officers representative of such members who have been elected by secret ballot.

(e) In any election required by this section which is to be held by secret ballot a reasonable opportunity shall be given for the nomination of candidates and every member in good standing shall be eligible to be a candidate and to hold office (subject to section 504 and to reasonable qualifications uniformly imposed) and shall have the right to vote for or otherwise support the candidate or candidates of his choice, without being subject to penalty, discipline, or improper interference or reprisal of any kind by such organization or any member thereof. Not less than fifteen days prior to the election notice thereof shall be mailed to each member at his last known home address. Each member in good standing shall be entitled to one vote. No member whose dues have been withheld by his employer for payment to such organization pursuant to his voluntary authorization provided for in a collective bargaining agreement shall be declared ineligible to vote or be a candidate for office in such organization by reason of alleged delay or default in the payment of dues. The votes cast by members of each local labor organization shall be counted, and the results published, separately. The election officials designated in the constitution and bylaws or the secretary, if no other official is designated, shall preserve for one year the ballots and all other records pertaining to the election. The election shall be conducted in accordance with the constitution and bylaws of such organization insofar as they are not inconsistent with the provisions of this title.

(f) When officers are chosen by a convention of delegates elected by secret ballot, the convention shall be conducted in accordance with the constitution and bylaws of the labor organization insofar as they are not inconsistent with the provisions of this title. The officials designated in the constitution and bylaws or the secretary, if no other is designated, shall preserve for one year the credentials of the delegates and all minutes and other records of the convention pertaining to the election of officers.

(g) No moneys received by any labor organization by way of dues, assessment, or similar levy, and no moneys of an employer shall be contributed or applied to promote the candidacy of any person in an election subject to the provisions of this title. Such moneys of a labor organization may be utilized for notices, factual statements of issues not involving candidates, and other expenses necessary for the holding of an election.

(h) If the Secretary, upon application of any member of a local labor organization, finds after hearing in accordance with the Administrative Procedure Act that the constitution and bylaws of such labor organization do not provide an adequate procedure for the removal of an elected officer guilty of serious misconduct, such officer may be removed, for cause shown and after notice and hearing, by the members in good standing voting in a secret ballot conducted by the officers of such labor organization in accordance with its constitution and bylaws insofar as they are not inconsistent with the provisions of this title.

(i) The Secretary shall promulgate rules and regulations prescribing minimum standards and procedures for determining the adequacy of the removal procedures to which reference is made in subsection (h).

ENFORCEMENT

SEC. 402.

(a) A member of a labor organization —

(1) who has exhausted the remedies available under the constitution and bylaws of such organization and of any parent body, or

(2) who has invoked such available remedies without obtaining a final decision within three calendar months after their invocation, may file a complaint with the secretary within one calendar month thereafter alleging the violation of any provision of section 401 (including violation of the constitution and bylaws of the labor organization pertaining to the election and removal of officers). The challenged election shall be presumed valid pending a final decision thereon (as hereinafter provided) and in the interim the affairs of the organization shall be conducted by the officers elected or in such other manner as its constitution and bylaws may provide.

(b) The Secretary shall investigate such complaint and, if he finds probable cause to believe that a violation of this title has occurred and has not been remedied, he shall, within sixty days after the filing of such complaint, bring a civil action against the labor organization as an entity in the district court of the United States in which such labor organization maintains its principal office to set aside the invalid election, if any, and to direct the conduct of an election or hearing and vote upon the removal of officers under the supervision of the Secretary and in accordance with the provisions of this title and such rules and regulations as the Secretary may prescribe. The court shall have power to take such action as it deems proper to preserve the assets of the labor organization.

(c) If, upon a preponderance of the evidence after a trial upon the merits, the court finds —

(1) that an election has not been held within the time prescribed by section 401, or

(2) that the violation of section 401 may have affected the outcome of an election, he court shall declare the election, if any, to be void and direct the conduct of a new election under supervision of the Secretary and, so far as lawful and practicable, in conformity with the constitution and bylaws of the labor organization. The Secretary shall promptly certify to the court the names of the persons elected, and the court shall thereupon enter a decree declaring such persons to be the officers of the labor organization. If the proceeding is for the removal of officers pursuant to subsection (h) of section 401, the Secretary shall certify the results of the vote and the court shall enter a decree declaring whether such persons have been removed as officers of the labor organization.

(d) An order directing an election, dismissing a complaint, or designating elected officers of a labor organization shall be appealable in the same manner as the final judgment in a civil action, but an order directing an election shall not be stayed pending appeal. . . .

PROHIBITION ON CERTAIN DISCIPLINE BY LABOR ORGANIZATION

SEC. 609. It shall be unlawful for any labor organization, or any officer, agent, shop steward, or other representative of a labor organization, or any employee thereof to fine, suspend, expel, or otherwise discipline any of its members for exercising any right to which he is entitled under the provisions of this Act. The provisions of section 102 shall be applicable in the enforcement of this section. . . .

OHIO PUBLIC SECTOR LABOR STATUTE, OHIO REVISED CODE

OHIO REVISED CODE

4117.01 Public employees' collective bargaining definitions.

As used in this chapter:

(A) "Person," in addition to those included in division (C) of section 1.59 of the Revised Code, includes employee organizations, public employees, and public employers.

(B) "Public employer" means the state or any political subdivision of the state located entirely within the state, including, without limitation, any municipal corporation with a population of at least five thousand according to the most recent federal decennial census; county; township with a population of at least five thousand in the unincorporated area of the township according to the most recent federal decennial census; school district; governing authority of a community school established under Chapter 3314. of the Revised Code; college preparatory boarding school established under Chapter 3328. of the Revised Code or its operator; state institution of higher learning; public or special district; state agency, authority, commission, or board; or other branch of public employment. "Public employer" does not include the nonprofit corporation formed under section 187.01 of the Revised Code.

(C) "Public employee" means any person holding a position by appointment or employment in the service of a public employer, including any person working pursuant to a contract between a public employer and a private employer and over whom the national labor relations board has declined jurisdiction on the basis that the involved employees are employees of a public employer, except:

(1) Persons holding elective office;

(2) Employees of the general assembly and employees of any other legislative body of the public employer whose principal duties are directly related to the legislative functions of the body;

(3) Employees on the staff of the governor or the chief executive of the public employer whose principal duties are directly related to the performance of the executive functions of the governor or the chief executive;

(4) Persons who are members of the Ohio organized militia, while training or performing duty under section 5919.29 or 5923.12 of the Revised Code;

(5) Employees of the state employment relations board, including those employees of the state employment relations board utilized by the state personnel board of review in the exercise of the powers and the performance of the duties and functions of the state personnel board of review;

(6) Confidential employees;

(7) Management level employees;

(8) Employees and officers of the courts, assistants to the attorney general,

assistant prosecuting attorneys, and employees of the clerks of courts who perform a judicial function;

(9) Employees of a public official who act in a fiduciary capacity, appointed pursuant to section 124.11 of the Revised Code;

(10) Supervisors;

(11) Students whose primary purpose is educational training, including graduate assistants or associates, residents, interns, or other students working as part-time public employees less than fifty per cent of the normal year in the employee's bargaining unit;

(12) Employees of county boards of election;

(13) Seasonal and casual employees as determined by the state employment relations board;

(14) Part-time faculty members of an institution of higher education;

(15) Participants in a work activity, developmental activity, or alternative work activity under sections 5107.40 to 5107.69 of the Revised Code who perform a service for a public employer that the public employer needs but is not performed by an employee of the public employer if the participant is not engaged in paid employment or subsidized employment pursuant to the activity;

(16) Employees included in the career professional service of the department of transportation under section 5501.20 of the Revised Code;

(17) Employees of community-based correctional facilities and district community-based correctional facilities created under sections 2301.51 to 2301.58 of the Revised Code who are not subject to a collective bargaining agreement on June 1, 2005.

(D) "Employee organization" means any labor or bona fide organization in which public employees participate and that exists for the purpose, in whole or in part, of dealing with public employers concerning grievances, labor disputes, wages, hours, terms, and other conditions of employment.

(E) "Exclusive representative" means the employee organization certified or recognized as an exclusive representative under section 4117.05 of the Revised Code.

(F) "Supervisor" means any individual who has authority, in the interest of the public employer, to hire, transfer, suspend, lay off, recall, promote, discharge, assign, reward, or discipline other public employees; to responsibly direct them; to adjust their grievances; or to effectively recommend such action, if the exercise of that authority is not of a merely routine or clerical nature, but requires the use of independent judgment, provided that:

(1) Employees of school districts who are department chairpersons or consulting teachers shall not be deemed supervisors;

(2) With respect to members of a police or fire department, no person shall

be deemed a supervisor except the chief of the department or those individuals who, in the absence of the chief, are authorized to exercise the authority and perform the duties of the chief of the department. Where prior to June 1, 1982, a public employer pursuant to a judicial decision, rendered in litigation to which the public employer was a party, has declined to engage in collective bargaining with members of a police or fire department on the basis that those members are supervisors, those members of a police or fire department do not have the rights specified in this chapter for the purposes of future collective bargaining. The state employment relations board shall decide all disputes concerning the application of division (F)(2) of this section.

(3) With respect to faculty members of a state institution of higher education, heads of departments or divisions are supervisors; however, no other faculty member or group of faculty members is a supervisor solely because the faculty member or group of faculty members participate in decisions with respect to courses, curriculum, personnel, or other matters of academic policy;

(4) No teacher as defined in section 3319.09 of the Revised Code shall be designated as a supervisor or a management level employee unless the teacher is employed under a contract governed by section 3319.01, 3319.011, or 3319.02 of the Revised Code and is assigned to a position for which a license deemed to be for administrators under state board rules is required pursuant to section 3319.22 of the Revised Code.

(G) "To bargain collectively" means to perform the mutual obligation of the public employer, by its representatives, and the representatives of its employees to negotiate in good faith at reasonable times and places with respect to wages, hours, terms, and other conditions of employment and the continuation, modification, or deletion of an existing provision of a collective bargaining agreement, with the intention of reaching an agreement, or to resolve questions arising under the agreement. "To bargain collectively" includes executing a written contract incorporating the terms of any agreement reached. The obligation to bargain collectively does not mean that either party is compelled to agree to a proposal nor does it require the making of a concession.

(H) "Strike" means continuous concerted action in failing to report to duty; willful absence from one's position; or stoppage of work in whole from the full, faithful, and proper performance of the duties of employment, for the purpose of inducing, influencing, or coercing a change in wages, hours, terms, and other conditions of employment. "Strike" does not include a stoppage of work by employees in good faith because of dangerous or unhealthful working conditions at the place of employment that are abnormal to the place of employment.

(I) "Unauthorized strike" includes, but is not limited to, concerted action during the term or extended term of a collective bargaining agreement or during the pendency of the settlement procedures set forth in section 4117.14 of the Revised Code in failing to report to duty; willful absence from one's position; stoppage of work; slowdown, or abstinence in whole or in part from the full, faithful, and proper performance of the duties of employment for the purpose of inducing, influencing, or coercing a change in wages, hours, terms, and other conditions of employment. "Unauthorized strike" includes any such action, absence, stoppage, slowdown, or abstinence when done partially or intermittently, whether during or after the expiration of the term or extended term of a collective bargaining agreement or during or after the pendency of the settlement procedures set forth in section 4117.14 of the Revised Code.

(J) "Professional employee" means any employee engaged in work that is predominantly intellectual, involving the consistent exercise of discretion and judgment in its performance and requiring knowledge of an advanced type in a field of science or learning customarily acquired by a prolonged course in an institution of higher learning or a hospital, as distinguished from a general academic education or from an apprenticeship; or an employee who has completed the courses of specialized intellectual instruction and is performing related work under the supervision of a professional person to become qualified as a professional employee.

(K) "Confidential employee" means any employee who works in the personnel offices of a public employer and deals with information to be used by the public employer in collective bargaining; or any employee who works in a close continuing relationship with public officers or representatives directly participating in collective bargaining on behalf of the employer.

(L) "Management level employee" means an individual who formulates policy on behalf of the public employer, who responsibly directs the implementation of policy, or who may reasonably be required on behalf of the public employer to assist in the preparation for the conduct of collective negotiations, administer collectively negotiated agreements, or have a major role in personnel administration. Assistant superintendents, principals, and assistant principals whose employment is governed by section 3319.02 of the Revised Code are management level employees. With respect to members of a faculty of a state institution of higher education, no person is a management level employee because of the person's involvement in the formulation or implementation of academic or institution policy.

(M) "Wages" means hourly rates of pay, salaries, or other forms of compensation for services rendered.

(N) "Member of a police department" means a person who is in the employ of a police department of a municipal corporation as a full-time regular police officer as the result of an appointment from a duly established civil service eligibility list or under section 737.15 or 737.16 of the Revised Code, a full-time deputy sheriff appointed under section 311.04 of the Revised Code, a township constable appointed under section 509.01 of the Revised Code, or a member of a township or joint police district police department appointed under section 505.49 of the Revised Code.

(O) "Members of the state highway patrol" means highway patrol troopers and radio operators appointed under section 5503.01 of the Revised Code.

(P) "Member of a fire department" means a person who is in the employ of a fire department of a municipal corporation or a township as a fire cadet, full-time regular firefighter, or promoted rank as the result of an appointment from a duly established civil service eligibility list or under section 505.38, 709.012, or 737.22 of the Revised Code.

(Q) "Day" means calendar day.

Amended by 129th General Assembly File No. 28, HB 153, § 101.01, eff. 9/29/2011.

Amended by 129th General Assembly File No. 1, HB 1, § 1, eff. 2/18/2011.

Amended by 128th General Assembly File No. 9, HB 1, (Vetoed Provisions) §101.01, eff. 10/16/2009 and 7/17/2009.

Effective Date: 12-13-2002; 12-30-2004; 06-27-2005; 03-30-2006; 10-12-2006

See 128th General Assembly File No. 9, HB 1, §812.30.

The amendment to this section by 129th General Assembly File No. 10, SB 5, § 1 was rejected by voters in the November, 2011 election.

4117.02 State employment relations board.

(A) There is hereby created the state employment relations board, consisting of three members to be appointed by the governor with the advice and consent of the senate. Members shall be knowledgeable about labor relations or personnel practices. No more than two of the three members shall belong to the same political party. A member of the state employment relations board during the member's period of service shall hold no other public office or public or private employment and shall allow no other responsibilities to interfere or conflict with the member's duties as a full-time state employment relations board member. Of the initial appointments made to the state employment relations board, one shall be for a term ending October 6, 1984, one shall be for a term ending October 6, 1985, and one shall be for a term ending October 6, 1986. Thereafter, terms of office shall be for six years, each term ending on the same day of the same month of the year as did the term that it succeeds. Each member shall hold office from the date of the member's appointment until the end of the term for which the member is appointed. Any member appointed to fill a vacancy occurring prior to the expiration of the term for which the member's predecessor was appointed shall hold office for the remainder of the term. Any member shall continue in office subsequent to the expiration of the member's term until the member's successor takes office or until a period of sixty days has elapsed, whichever occurs first. The governor may remove any member of the state employment relations board, upon notice and public hearing, for neglect of duty or malfeasance in office, but for no other cause.

(B) (1) The governor shall designate one member of the state employment relations board to serve as chairperson of the state employment relations board. The chairperson is the head of the state employment relations board and its chief executive officer.

(2) The chairperson shall exercise all administrative powers and duties conferred upon the state employment relations board under this chapter and shall do all of the following:

(a) Employ, promote, supervise, and remove all employees of the state employment relations board, and establish, change, or abolish positions and assign or reassign the duties of those employees as the chairperson determines necessary to achieve the most efficient performance of the duties of the state employment relations board under this chapter;

(b) Determine the utilization by the state personnel board of review of employees of the state employment relations board as necessary for the state personnel board of review to exercise the powers and perform the duties of the state personnel board of review.

(c) Maintain the office of the state employment relations board in Columbus and manage the office's daily operations, including securing offices, facilities, equipment, and supplies necessary to house the state employment relations board, employees of the state employment relations board, the state personnel board of review, and files and records under the control of the state employment relations board and under the control of the state personnel board of review;

(d) Prepare and submit to the office of budget and management a budget for each biennium according to section 107.03 of the Revised Code, and include in the budget the costs of the state employment relations board and its staff and the costs of the state employment relations board in discharging any duty imposed by law upon the state employment relations board, the chairperson, or any of the employees or agents of the state employment relations board, and the costs of the state personnel board of review in discharging any duty imposed by law on the state personnel board of review or an agent of the state personnel board of review.

(C) The vacancy on the state employment relations board does not impair the right of the remaining members to exercise all the powers of the state employment relations board, and two members of the state employment relations board, at all times, constitute a quorum. The state employment relations board shall have an official seal of which courts shall take judicial notice.

(D) The state employment relations board shall make an annual report in writing to the governor and to the general assembly, stating in detail the work it has done.

(E) Compensation of the chairperson and members shall be in accordance with division (J) of section 124.15 of the Revised Code. The chairperson and the members are eligible for reappointment. In addition to such compensation, all members shall be reimbursed for their necessary expenses incurred in the performance of their work as members.

(F) (1) The chairperson, after consulting with the other state employment relations board members and receiving the consent of at least one other board member, shall appoint an executive director. The chairperson also shall appoint attorneys and shall appoint an assistant executive director who shall be an attorney admitted to practice law in this state and who shall serve as a liaison to the attorney general on legal matters before the state employment relations board.

(2) The state employment relations board shall appoint members of fact-finding panels and shall prescribe their job duties.

(G) (1) The executive director shall serve at the pleasure of the chairperson. The executive director, under the direction of the chairperson, shall do all of the following:

(a) Act as chief administrative officer for the state employment relations board;

(b) Ensure that all employees of the state employment relations board comply with the rules of the state employment relations board;

(c) Do all things necessary for the efficient and effective implementation of the duties of the state employment relations board.

(2) The duties of the executive director described in division (G)(1) of this section do not relieve the chairperson from final responsibility for the proper performance of the duties described in that division.

(H) The attorney general shall be the legal adviser of the state employment relations board and shall appear for and represent the state employment relations board and its agents in all legal proceedings. The state employment relations board may utilize regional, local, or other agencies, and utilize voluntary and uncompensated services as needed. The state employment relations board may contract with the federal mediation and conciliation service for the assistance of mediators, arbitrators, and other personnel the service makes available. The chairperson shall appoint all employees on the basis of training, practical experience, education, and character, notwithstanding the requirements established by section 119.09 of the Revised Code. The chairperson shall give special regard to the practical training and experience that employees have for the particular position involved. The executive director, assistant executive director, administrative law judges, employees holding a fiduciary or administrative relation to the state employment relations board as described in division (A)(9) of section 124.11 of the Revised Code, and the personal secretaries and assistants of the state employment relations board members are in the unclassified service. All other full-time employees of the state employment relations board are in the classified service. All employees of the state employment relations board shall be paid in accordance with Chapter 12 of the Revised Code.

(I) The chairperson shall select and assign administrative law judges and other agents whose functions are to conduct hearings with due regard to their impartiality, judicial temperament, and knowledge. If in any proceeding under this chapter, any party prior to five days before the hearing thereto files with the state employment relations board a sworn statement charging that the administrative law judge or other agent designated to conduct the hearing is biased or partial in the proceeding, the state employment relations board may disqualify the person and designate another administrative law judge or agent to conduct the proceeding. At least ten days before any hearing, the state employment relations board shall notify all parties to a proceeding of the name of the administrative law judge or agent designated to conduct the hearing.

(J) The principal office of the state employment relations board is in Columbus, but it may meet and exercise any or all of its powers at any other place within the state. The state employment relations board may, by one or more of its employees, or any agents or agencies it designates, conduct in any part of this state any proceeding, hearing, investigation, inquiry, or election necessary to the performance of its functions; provided, that no person so designated may later sit in determination of an appeal of the decision of that cause or matter.

(K) In addition to the powers and functions provided in other sections of this chapter, the state employment relations board shall do all of the following:

(1) Create a bureau of mediation within the state employment relations board, to perform the functions provided in section 4117.14 of the Revised Code. This bureau shall also establish, after consulting representatives of employee organizations and public employers, panels of qualified persons to be available to serve as members of fact-finding panels and arbitrators.

(2) Conduct studies of problems involved in representation and negotiation and make recommendations for legislation;

(3) Hold hearings pursuant to this chapter and, for the purpose of the hearings and inquiries, administer oaths and affirmations, examine witnesses and documents, take testimony and receive evidence, compel the attendance of witnesses and the production of documents by the issuance of subpoenas, and delegate these powers to any members of the state employment relations board or any administrative law judge employed by the state employment relations board for the performance of its functions;

(4) Train representatives of employee organizations and public employers in the rules and techniques of collective bargaining procedures;

(5) Make studies and analyses of, and act as a clearinghouse of information relating to, conditions of employment of public employees throughout the state and request assistance, services, and data from any public employee organization, public employer, or governmental unit. Public employee organizations, public employers, and governmental units shall provide such assistance, services, and data as will enable the state employment relations board to carry out its functions and powers.

(6) Make available to employee organizations, public employers, mediators, fact-finding panels, arbitrators, and joint study committees statistical data relating to wages, benefits, and employment practices in public and private employment applicable to various localities and occupations to assist them to resolve issues in negotiations;

(7) Notwithstanding section 119.13 of the Revised Code, establish standards of persons who practice before it;

(8) Adopt, amend, and rescind rules and procedures and exercise other powers appropriate to carry out this chapter. Before the adoption, amendment, or rescission of rules and procedures under this section, the state employment relations board shall do all of the following:

(a) Maintain a list of interested public employers and employee organizations and mail notice to such groups of any proposed rule or procedure, amendment thereto, or rescission thereof at least thirty days before any public hearing thereon;

(b) Mail a copy of each proposed rule or procedure, amendment thereto, or rescission thereof to any person who requests a copy within five days after receipt of the request therefor;

(c) Consult with appropriate statewide organizations representing public employers or employees who would be affected by the proposed rule or procedure.

Although the state employment relations board is expected to discharge these duties diligently, failure to mail any notice or copy, or to so consult with any person, is not jurisdictional and shall not be construed to invalidate any proceeding or action of the state employment relations board.

(L) In case of neglect or refusal to obey a subpoena issued to any person, the court of common pleas of the county in which the investigation or the public hearing occurs, upon application by the state employment relations board, may issue an order requiring the person to appear before the state employment relations board and give testimony about the matter under investigation. The court may punish a failure to obey the order as contempt.

(M) Any subpoena, notice of hearing, or other process or notice of the state employment relations board issued under this section may be served personally, by certified mail, or by leaving a copy at the principal office or personal residence of the respondent required to be served. A return, made and verified by the individual making the service and setting forth the manner of service, is proof of service, and a return post office receipt, when certified mail is used, is proof of service. All process in any court to which application is made under this chapter may be served in the county wherein the persons required to be served reside or are found.

(N) All expenses of the state employment relations board, including all necessary traveling and subsistence expenses incurred by the members or employees of the state employment relations board under its orders, shall be paid pursuant to itemized vouchers approved by the chairperson of the state employment relations board, the executive director, or both, or such other person as the chairperson designates for that purpose.

(O) Whenever the state employment relations board determines that a substantial controversy exists with respect to the application or interpretation of this chapter and the matter is of public or great general interest, the state employment relations board shall certify its final order directly to the court of appeals having jurisdiction over the area in which the principal office of the public employer directly affected by the application or interpretation is located. The chairperson shall file with the clerk of the court a certified copy of the transcript of the proceedings before the state employment relations board pertaining to the final order. If upon hearing and consideration the court decides that the final order of the state employment relations board is unlawful or is not supported by substantial evidence on the record as a whole, the court shall reverse and vacate the final order or modify it and enter final judgment in accordance with the modification; otherwise, the court shall affirm the final order. The notice of the final order of the state employment relations board to the interested parties shall contain a certification by the chairperson of the state employment relations board that the final order is of public or great general interest and that a certified transcript of the record of the proceedings before the state employment relations board had been filed with the clerk of the court as an appeal to the court. For the purposes of this division, the state employment relations board has standing to bring its final order properly before the court of appeals.

(P) Except as otherwise specifically provided in this section, the state employment relations board is subject to Chapter 119. of the Revised Code, including the procedure for submission of proposed rules to the general assembly for legislative review under division (H) of section 119.03 of the Revised Code.

Amended by 128th General Assembly File No. 9, HB 1, § 101.01, eff. 7/17/2009.

Effective Date: 09-26-2003

The amendment to this section by 129th General Assembly File No. 10, SB 5, § 1 was rejected by voters in the November, 2011 election.

4117.03   Rights of public employees.

(A) Public employees have the right to:

(1) Form, join, assist, or participate in, or refrain from forming, joining, assisting, or participating in, except as otherwise provided in Chapter 4117. of the Revised Code, any employee organization of their own choosing;

(2) Engage in other concerted activities for the purpose of collective bargaining or other mutual aid and protection;

(3) Representation by an employee organization;

(4) Bargain collectively with their public employers to determine wages, hours, terms and other conditions of employment and the continuation, modification, or deletion of an existing provision of a collective bargaining agreement, and enter into collective bargaining agreements;

(5) Present grievances and have them adjusted, without the intervention of the bargaining representative, as long as the adjustment is not inconsistent with the terms of the collective bargaining agreement then in effect and as long as the bargaining representatives have the opportunity to be present at the adjustment.

(B) Persons on active duty or acting in any capacity as members of the organized militia do not have collective bargaining rights.

(C) Except as provided in division (D) of this section, nothing in Chapter 4117. of the Revised Code prohibits public employers from electing to engage in collective bargaining, to meet and confer, to hold discussions, or to engage in any other form of collective negotiations with public employees who are not subject to Chapter 4117. of the Revised Code pursuant to division (C) of section 4117.01 of the Revised Code.

(D) A public employer shall not engage in collective bargaining or other forms of collective negotiations with the employees of county boards of elections referred to in division (C)(12) of section 4117.01 of the Revised Code.

(E) Employees of public schools may bargain collectively for health care benefits.

Amended by 129th General Assembly File No. 28, HB 153, § 101.01, eff. 9/29/2011.

Amended by 129th General Assembly File No. 39, SB 171, § 1, eff. 6/30/2011.

Effective Date: 04-01-1984; 05-07-2004; 09-29-2005; 2007 HB119 09-29-2007

The amendment to this section by 129th General Assembly File No. 10, SB 5, § 1 was rejected by voters in the November, 2011 election.

4117.04   Public employers exclusive representative.

(A) Public employers shall extend to an exclusive representative designated under section 4117.05 of the Revised Code, the right to represent exclusively the employees in the appropriate bargaining unit and the right to unchallenged and exclusive representation for a period of not less than twelve months following the date of certification and thereafter, if the public employer and the employee organization enter into an agreement, for a period of not more than three years from the date of signing the agreement. For the purposes of this section, extensions of agreements shall not be construed to affect the expiration date of the original agreement.

(B) A public employer shall bargain collectively with an exclusive representative designated under section 4117.05 of the Revised Code for purposes of Chapter 4117. of the Revised Code.

When the state employment relations board notifies a public employer that it has certified an employee organization as exclusive representative for a unit of its employees, the public employer shall designate an employer representative and promptly notify the board and the employee organization of his identity and address. On certification, the employee organization shall designate an employee representative and promptly notify the board and the public employer of his identity and address. The board or any party shall address to the appropriate designated representative all communications concerned with collective relationships under Chapter 4117. of the Revised Code. In the case of municipal corporations, counties, school districts, educational service centers, villages, and townships, the designation of the employer representative is as provided in division (C) of section 4117.10 of the Revised Code. The designated representative of a party may sign agreements resulting from collective bargaining on behalf of his designator; but the agreements are subject to the procedures set forth in Chapter 4117. of the Revised Code.

Effective Date: 09-29-1995

4117.05   Employee organization to become exclusive representative — procedure.

(A) An employee organization becomes the exclusive representative of all the public employees in an appropriate unit for the purposes of collective bargaining by either:

(1) Being certified by the state employment relations board when a majority of the voting employees in the unit select the employee organization as their representative in a board-conducted election under section 4117.07 of the Revised Code;

(2) Filing a request with a public employer with a copy to the state employment relations board for recognition as an exclusive representative. In the request for recognition, the employee organization shall describe the bargaining unit, shall allege that a majority of the employees in the bargaining unit wish to be represented by the employee organization, and shall support the request with substantial evidence based on, and in accordance with, rules prescribed by the board demonstrating that a majority of the employees in the bargaining unit wish to be represented by the employee organization. Immediately upon receipt of a request, the public employer shall either request an election under division (A)(2) of section 4117.07 of the Revised Code, or take the following action:

(a) Post notice in each facility at which employees in the proposed unit are employed, setting forth the description of the bargaining unit, the name of the employee organization requesting recognition, and the date of the request for recognition, and advising employees that objections to certification must be filed with the state employment relations board not later than the twenty-first day following the date of the request for recognition;

(b) Immediately notify the state employment relations board of the request for recognition.

The state employment relations board shall certify the employee organization filing the request for recognition on the twenty-second day following the filing of the request for recognition, unless by the twenty-first day following the filing of the request for recognition it receives:

(i) A petition for an election from the public employer pursuant to division (A)(2) of section 4117.07 of the Revised Code;

(ii) Substantial evidence based on, and in accordance with, rules prescribed by the board demonstrating that a majority of the employees in the described bargaining unit do not wish to be represented by the employee organization filing the request for recognition;

(iii) Substantial evidence based on, and in accordance with, rules prescribed by the board from another employee organization demonstrating that at least ten percent of the employees in the described bargaining unit wish to be represented by such other employee organization; or

(iv) Substantial evidence based on, and in accordance with, rules prescribed by the board indicating that the proposed unit is not an appropriate unit pursuant to section 4117.06 of the Revised Code.

(B) Nothing in this section shall be construed to permit a public employer to recognize, or the state employment relations board to certify, an employee organization as an exclusive representative under Chapter 4117. of the Revised Code if there is in effect a lawful written agreement, contract, or memorandum of understanding between the public employer and another employee organization which, on the effective date of this section, has been recognized by a public employer as the exclusive representative of the employees in a unit or which by tradition, custom, practice, election, or negotiation has been the only employee organization representing all employees in the unit; this restriction does not apply to that period of time covered by any agreement which exceeds three years. For the purposes of this section, extensions of agreement do not affect the expiration of the original agreement.

Effective Date: 04-01-1984

The amendment to this section by 129th General Assembly File No. 10, SB 5, § 1 was rejected by voters in the November, 2011 election.

4117.06 State employment relations board to determine collective bargaining unit.

(A) The state employment relations board shall decide in each case the unit appropriate for the purposes of collective bargaining. The determination is final and conclusive and not appealable to the court.

(B) The board shall determine the appropriateness of each bargaining unit and shall consider among other relevant factors: the desires of the employees; the community of interest; wages, hours, and other working conditions of the public employees; the effect of over-fragmentation; the efficiency of operations of the public employer; the administrative structure of the public employer; and the history of collective bargaining.

(C) The board may determine a unit to be the appropriate unit in a particular case, even though some other unit might also be appropriate.

(D) In addition, in determining the appropriate unit, the board shall not:

(1) Decide that any unit is appropriate if the unit includes both professional and nonprofessional employees, unless a majority of the professional employees and a majority of the nonprofessional employees first vote for inclusion in the unit;

(2) Include guards or correction officers at correctional or mental institutions, special police officers appointed in accordance with sections 5119.14 and 5123.13 of the Revised Code, psychiatric attendants employed at mental health forensic facilities, youth leaders employed at juvenile correction facilities, or any public employee employed as a guard to enforce against other employees rules to protect property of the employer or to protect the safety of persons on the employer's premises in a unit with other employees;

(3) Include members of a police or fire department or members of the state highway patrol in a unit with other classifications of public employees of the department;

(4) Designate as appropriate a bargaining unit that contains more than one institution of higher education; nor shall it within any such institution of higher education designate as appropriate a unit where such designation would be inconsistent with the accreditation standards or interpretations of such standards, governing such institution of higher education or any department, school, or college thereof. For the purposes of this division, any branch or regional campus of a public institution of higher education is part of that institution of higher education.

(5) Designate as appropriate a bargaining unit that contains employees within

the jurisdiction of more than one elected county office holder, unless the county-elected office holder and the board of county commissioners agree to such other designation;

(6) With respect to members of a police department, designate as appropriate a unit that includes rank and file members of the department with members who are of the rank of sergeant or above;

(7) Except as otherwise provided by division (A)(3) of section 3314.10 or division (B) of section 3326.18 of the Revised Code, designate as appropriate a bargaining unit that contains employees from multiple community schools established under Chapter 3314. or multiple science, technology, engineering, and mathematics schools established under Chapter 3326. of the Revised Code. For purposes of this division, more than one unit may be designated within a single community school or science, technology, engineering, and mathematics school.

This section shall not be deemed to prohibit multiunit bargaining.

Effective Date: 06-30-1997; 2007 HB119 09-29-2007

The amendment to this section by 129th General Assembly File No. 10, SB 5, § 1 was rejected by voters in the November, 2011 election.

4117.07   Procedure upon filing petition for election.

(A) When a petition is filed, in accordance with rules prescribed by the state employment relations board:

(1) By any employee or group of employees, or any individual or employee organization acting in their behalf, alleging that at least thirty per cent of the employees in an appropriate unit wish to be represented for collective bargaining by an exclusive representative, or asserting that the designated exclusive representative is no longer the representative of the majority of employees in the unit, the board shall investigate the petition, and if it has reasonable cause to believe that a question of representation exists, provide for an appropriate hearing upon due notice to the parties;

(2) By the employer alleging that one or more employee organizations has presented to it a claim to be recognized as the exclusive representative in an appropriate unit, the board shall investigate the petition, and if it has reasonable cause to believe that a question of representation exists, provide for an appropriate hearing upon due notice to the parties.

If the board finds upon the record of a hearing that a question of representation exists, it shall direct an election and certify the results thereof. No one may vote in an election by proxy. The board may also certify an employee organization as an exclusive representative if it determines that a free and untrammeled election cannot be conducted because of the employer's unfair labor practices and that at one time the employee organization had the support of the majority of the employees in the unit.

(B) Only the names of those employee organizations designated by more than ten per cent of the employees in the unit found to be appropriate may be placed on the ballot. Nothing in this section shall be construed to prohibit the waiving of hearings by stipulation, in conformity with the rules of the board, for the purpose of a consent election.

(C) The board shall conduct representation elections by secret ballot cast, at the board's discretion, by mail or electronically or in person, and at times and places selected by the board subject to the following:

(1) The board shall give no less than ten days' notice of the time and place of an election;

(2) The board shall establish rules concerning the conduct of any election including, but not limited to, rules to guarantee the secrecy of the ballot;

(3) The board may not certify a representative unless the representative receives a majority of the valid ballots cast;

(4) Except as provided in this section, the board shall include on the ballot a choice of "no representative";

(5) In an election where none of the choices on the ballot receives a majority, the board shall conduct a runoff election. In that case, the ballot shall provide for a selection between the two choices or parties receiving the highest and the second highest number of ballots cast in the election.

(6) The board may not conduct an election under this section in any appropriate bargaining unit within which a board-conducted election was held in the preceding twelve-month period, nor during the term of any lawful collective bargaining agreement between a public employer and an exclusive representative.

Petitions for elections may be filed with the board no sooner than one hundred twenty days or later than ninety days before the expiration date of any collective bargaining agreement, or after the expiration date, until the public employer and exclusive representative enter into a new written agreement.

For the purposes of this section, extensions of agreements do not affect the expiration date of the original agreement.

Amended by 128th General Assembly File No. 9, HB 1, § 101.01, eff. 10/16/2009.

Effective Date: 04-01-1984

The amendment to this section by 129th General Assembly File No. 10, SB 5, § 1 was rejected by voters in the November, 2011 election.

4117.08   Matters subject to collective bargaining.

(A) All matters pertaining to wages, hours, or terms and other conditions of employment and the continuation, modification, or deletion of an existing provision of a collective bargaining agreement are subject to collective bargaining between the public employer and the exclusive representative, except as otherwise specified in this section and division (E) of section 4117.03 of the Revised Code.

(B) The conduct and grading of civil service examinations, the rating of candidates, the establishment of eligible lists from the examinations, and the original appointments from the eligible lists are not appropriate subjects for collective bargaining.

(C) Unless a public employer agrees otherwise in a collective bargaining agreement, nothing in Chapter 4117. of the Revised Code impairs the right and responsibility of each public employer to:

(1) Determine matters of inherent managerial policy which include, but are not limited to areas of discretion or policy such as the functions and programs of the public employer, standards of services, its overall budget, utilization of technology, and organizational structure;

(2) Direct, supervise, evaluate, or hire employees;

(3) Maintain and improve the efficiency and effectiveness of governmental operations;

(4) Determine the overall methods, process, means, or personnel by which governmental operations are to be conducted;

(5) Suspend, discipline, demote, or discharge for just cause, or lay off, transfer, assign, schedule, promote, or retain employees;

(6) Determine the adequacy of the work force;

(7) Determine the overall mission of the employer as a unit of government;

(8) Effectively manage the work force;

(9) Take actions to carry out the mission of the public employer as a governmental unit.

The employer is not required to bargain on subjects reserved to the management and direction of the governmental unit except as affect wages, hours, terms and conditions of employment, and the continuation, modification, or deletion of an existing provision of a collective bargaining agreement. A public employee or exclusive representative may raise a legitimate complaint or file a grievance based on the collective bargaining agreement.

Effective Date: 04-01-1984; 09-29-2005; 2007 HB119 09-29-2007

The amendment to this section by 129th General Assembly File No. 10, SB 5, § 1 was rejected by voters in the November, 2011 election.

4117.09   Parties to execute written agreement — provisions of agreement.

(A) The parties to any collective bargaining agreement shall reduce the agreement to writing and both execute it.

(B) The agreement shall contain a provision that:

(1) Provides for a grievance procedure which may culminate with final and binding arbitration of unresolved grievances, and disputed interpretations of agreements, and which is valid and enforceable under its terms when entered into in accordance with this chapter. No publication thereof is required to make it effective. A party to the agreement may bring suits for violation of agreements

or the enforcement of an award by an arbitrator in the court of common pleas of any county wherein a party resides or transacts business.

(2) Authorizes the public employer to deduct the periodic dues, initiation fees, and assessments of members of the exclusive representative upon presentation of a written deduction authorization by the employee.

(C) The agreement may contain a provision that requires as a condition of employment, on or after a mutually agreed upon probationary period or sixty days following the beginning of employment, whichever is less, or the effective date of a collective bargaining agreement, whichever is later, that the employees in the unit who are not members of the employee organization pay to the employee organization a fair share fee. The arrangement does not require any employee to become a member of the employee organization, nor shall fair share fees exceed dues paid by members of the employee organization who are in the same bargaining unit. Any public employee organization representing public employees pursuant to this chapter shall prescribe an internal procedure to determine a rebate, if any, for nonmembers which conforms to federal law, provided a nonmember makes a timely demand on the employee organization. Absent arbitrary and capricious action, such determination is conclusive on the parties except that a challenge to the determination may be filed with the state employment relations board within thirty days of the determination date specifying the arbitrary or capricious nature of the determination and the board shall review the rebate determination and decide whether it was arbitrary or capricious. The deduction of a fair share fee by the public employer from the payroll check of the employee and its payment to the employee organization is automatic and does not require the written authorization of the employee.

The internal rebate procedure shall provide for a rebate of expenditures in support of partisan politics or ideological causes not germaine [germane] to the work of employee organizations in the realm of collective bargaining.

Any public employee who is a member of and adheres to established and traditional tenets or teachings of a bona fide religion or religious body which has historically held conscientious objections to joining or financially supporting an employee organization and which is exempt from taxation under the provisions of the Internal Revenue Code shall not be required to join or financially support any employee organization as a condition of employment. Upon submission of proper proof of religious conviction to the board, the board shall declare the employee exempt from becoming a member of or financially supporting an employee organization. The employee shall be required, in lieu of the fair share fee, to pay an amount of money equal to the fair share fee to a nonreligious charitable fund exempt from taxation under section 501(c)(3) of the Internal Revenue Code mutually agreed upon by the employee and the representative of the employee organization to which the employee would otherwise be required to pay the fair share fee. The employee shall furnish to the employee organization written receipts evidencing such payment, and failure to make the payment or furnish the receipts shall subject the employee to the same sanctions as would nonpayment of dues under the applicable collective bargaining agreement.

No public employer shall agree to a provision requiring that a public employee become a member of an employee organization as a condition for securing or retaining employment.

(D) As used in this division, "teacher" means any employee of a school district certified to teach in the public schools of this state.

The agreement may contain a provision that provides for a peer review plan under which teachers in a bargaining unit or representatives of an employee organization representing teachers may, for other teachers of the same bargaining unit or teachers whom the employee organization represents, participate in assisting, instructing, reviewing, evaluating, or appraising and make recommendations or participate in decisions with respect to the retention, discharge, renewal, or nonrenewal of, the teachers covered by a peer review plan.

The participation of teachers or their employee organization representative in a peer review plan permitted under this division shall not be construed as an unfair labor practice under this chapter or as a violation of any other provision of law or rule adopted pursuant thereto.

(E) No agreement shall contain an expiration date that is later than three years from the date of execution. The parties may extend any agreement, but the extensions do not affect the expiration date of the original agreement.

Effective Date: 03-01-1990

The amendment to this section by 129th General Assembly File No. 10, SB 5, § 1 was rejected by voters in the November, 2011 election.

4117.10   Terms of agreement.

(A) An agreement between a public employer and an exclusive representative entered into pursuant to this chapter governs the wages, hours, and terms and conditions of public employment covered by the agreement. If the agreement provides for a final and binding arbitration of grievances, public employers, employees, and employee organizations are subject solely to that grievance procedure and the state personnel board of review or civil service commissions have no jurisdiction to receive and determine any appeals relating to matters that were the subject of a final and binding grievance procedure. Where no agreement exists or where an agreement makes no specification about a matter, the public employer and public employees are subject to all applicable state or local laws or ordinances pertaining to the wages, hours, and terms and conditions of employment for public employees. Laws pertaining to civil rights, affirmative action, unemployment compensation, workers' compensation, the retirement of public employees, and residency requirements, the minimum educational requirements contained in the Revised Code pertaining to public education including the requirement of a certificate by the fiscal officer of a school district pursuant to section 5705.41 of the Revised Code, the provisions of division (A) of section 124.34 of the Revised Code governing the disciplining of officers and employees who have been convicted of a felony, and the minimum standards promulgated by the state board of education pursuant to division (D) of section 3301.07 of the Revised Code prevail over conflicting provisions of agreements between employee organizations and public employers. The law pertaining to the leave of absence and compensation provided under section 5923.05 of the Revised Code prevails over any conflicting provisions of such agreements if the terms of the agreement contain benefits which are less than those contained in that section or the agreement contains no such terms and the public authority is the state or any agency, authority, commission, or board of the state or if the public authority is another entity listed in division (B) of section 4117.01 of the Revised Code that elects to provide leave of absence and compensation as provided in section 5923.05 of the Revised Code. The law pertaining to the leave established under section 5906.02 of the Revised Code prevails over any conflicting provision of an agreement between an employee organization and public employer if the terms of the agreement contain benefits that are less than those contained in section 5906.02 of the Revised Code. Except for sections 306.08, 306.12, 306.35, and 4981.22 of the Revised Code and arrangements entered into thereunder, and section 4981.21 of the Revised Code as necessary to comply with section 13(c) of the "Urban Mass Transportation Act of 1964," 87 Stat. 295, 49 U.S.C.A. 1609(c), as amended, and arrangements entered into thereunder, this chapter prevails over any and all other conflicting laws, resolutions, provisions, present or future, except as otherwise specified in this chapter or as otherwise specified by the general assembly. Nothing in this section prohibits or shall be construed to invalidate the provisions of an agreement establishing supplemental workers' compensation or unemployment compensation benefits or exceeding minimum requirements contained in the Revised Code pertaining to public education or the minimum standards promulgated by the state board of education pursuant to division (D) of section 3301.07 of the Revised Code.

(B) The public employer shall submit a request for funds necessary to implement an agreement and for approval of any other matter requiring the approval of the appropriate legislative body to the legislative body within fourteen days of the date on which the parties finalize the agreement, unless otherwise specified, but if the appropriate legislative body is not in session at the time, then within fourteen days after it convenes. The legislative body must approve or reject the submission as a whole, and the submission is deemed approved if the legislative body fails to act within thirty days after the public employer submits the agreement. The parties may specify that those provisions of the agreement not requiring action by a legislative body are effective and operative in accordance with the terms of the agreement, provided there has been compliance with division (C) of this section. If the legislative body rejects the submission of the public employer, either party may reopen all or part of the entire agreement.

As used in this section, "legislative body" includes the governing board of a municipal corporation, school district, college or university, village, township, or board of county commissioners or any other body that has authority to approve the budget of their public jurisdiction and, with regard to the state, "legislative body" means the controlling board.

(C) The chief executive officer, or the chief executive officer's representative, of each municipal corporation, the designated representative of the board of education of each school district, college or university, or any other body that has authority to approve the budget of their public jurisdiction, the designated representative of the board of county commissioners and of each elected officeholder of the county whose employees are covered by the collective negotiations, and the designated representative of the village or the board of township trustees of each township is responsible for negotiations in the collective bargaining process; except that the legislative body may accept or reject a proposed collective bargaining agreement. When the matters about which there is agreement are reduced to writing and approved by the employee organization and the legislative body, the agreement is binding upon the legislative body, the employer, and the employee organization and employees covered by the agreement.

(D) There is hereby established an office of collective bargaining in the department of administrative services for the purpose of negotiating with and entering into written agreements between state agencies, departments, boards, and commissions and the exclusive representative on matters of wages, hours, terms and other conditions of employment and the continuation, modification, or deletion of an existing provision of a collective bargaining agreement. Nothing in any provision of law to the contrary shall be interpreted as excluding the bureau of workers' compensation and the industrial commission from the preceding sentence. This office shall not negotiate on behalf of other statewide elected officials or boards of trustees of state institutions of higher education who shall be considered as separate public employers for the purposes of this chapter; however, the office may negotiate on behalf of these officials or trustees where authorized by the officials or trustees. The staff of the office of collective bargaining are in the unclassified service. The director of administrative services shall fix the compensation of the staff.

The office of collective bargaining shall:

(1) Assist the director in formulating management's philosophy for public collective bargaining as well as planning bargaining strategies;

(2) Conduct negotiations with the exclusive representatives of each employee organization;

(3) Coordinate the state's resources in all mediation, fact-finding, and arbitration cases as well as in all labor disputes;

(4) Conduct systematic reviews of collective bargaining agreements for the purpose of contract negotiations;

(5) Coordinate the systematic compilation of data by all agencies that is required for negotiating purposes;

(6) Prepare and submit an annual report and other reports as requested to the governor and the general assembly on the implementation of this chapter and its impact upon state government.

Amended by 128th General Assembly File No. 29, HB 48, § 1, eff. 7/2/2010.

Effective Date: 03-22-1999; 09-29-2005

The amendment to this section by 129th General Assembly File No. 10, SB 5, § 1 was rejected by voters in the November, 2011 election.

4117.101   Prohibiting agreements contrary to community school provisions.

Notwithstanding sections 4117.08 and 4117.10 of the Revised Code, no agreement entered into under this chapter may contain any provision that in any way limits the effect or operation of Chapter 3314. of the Revised Code or limits the authority of a school district board of education, or the governing board of an educational service center described in division (C)(1)(d) of section 3314.02 of the Revised Code, to enter into a contract with a community school under that chapter. However, nothing in this section shall be construed to prohibit an agreement entered into under this chapter from containing requirements and procedures governing the reassignment of teachers who are employed in a school at the time it is converted to a community school pursuant to Chapter 3314. of the Revised Code and who do not choose or are not chosen to teach in that community school.

Effective Date: 04-08-2003

4117.102   List of school districts with agreements with teacher employee organizations.

The state employment relations board shall compile a list of the school districts in the state that have filed with the board agreements entered into with teacher employee organizations under this chapter. The board shall annually update the list to reflect, for each district, for the current fiscal year, the starting salary in the district for teachers with no prior teaching experience who hold bachelors degrees. The board shall send a copy of each annually updated list to the state board of education.

Effective Date: 09-05-2001

4117.103   Contract may not prohibit district board from utilizing volunteers.

Notwithstanding any provision of section 4117.08 or 4117.10 of the Revised Code to the contrary, no agreement entered into under this chapter on or after the effective date of this section shall prohibit a school district board of education from utilizing volunteers to assist the district and its schools in performing any of their functions, other than functions for which a license, permit, or certificate issued by the state board of education under section 3301.074 or Chapter 3319. of the Revised Code or a certificate issued under division (A) or (B) of section 3327.10 of the Revised Code is required.

Effective Date: 09-29-2005

4117.11   Unfair labor practice.

(A) It is an unfair labor practice for a public employer, its agents, or representatives to:

(1) Interfere with, restrain, or coerce employees in the exercise of the rights guaranteed in Chapter 4117. of the Revised Code or an employee organization in the selection of its representative for the purposes of collective bargaining or the adjustment of grievances;

(2) Initiate, create, dominate, or interfere with the formation or administration of any employee organization, or contribute financial or other support to it; except that a public employer may permit employees to confer with it during working hours without loss of time or pay, permit the exclusive representative to use the facilities of the public employer for membership or other meetings, or permit the exclusive representative to use the internal mail system or other

internal communications system;

(3) Discriminate in regard to hire or tenure of employment or any term or condition of employment on the basis of the exercise of rights guaranteed by Chapter 4117. of the Revised Code. Nothing precludes any employer from making and enforcing an agreement pursuant to division (C) of section 4117.09 of the Revised Code.

(4) Discharge or otherwise discriminate against an employee because he has filed charges or given testimony under Chapter 4117. of the Revised Code;

(5) Refuse to bargain collectively with the representative of his employees recognized as the exclusive representative or certified pursuant to Chapter 4117. of the Revised Code;

(6) Establish a pattern or practice of repeated failures to timely process grievances and requests for arbitration of grievances;

(7) Lock out or otherwise prevent employees from performing their regularly assigned duties where an object thereof is to bring pressure on the employees or an employee organization to compromise or capitulate to the employer's terms regarding a labor relations dispute;

(8) Cause or attempt to cause an employee organization, its agents, or representatives to violate division (B) of this section.

(B) It is an unfair labor practice for an employee organization, its agents, or representatives, or public employees to:

(1) Restrain or coerce employees in the exercise of the rights guaranteed in Chapter 4117. of the Revised Code. This division does not impair the right of an employee organization to prescribe its own rules with respect to the acquisition or retention of membership therein, or an employer in the selection of his representative for the purpose of collective bargaining or the adjustment of grievances.

(2) Cause or attempt to cause an employer to violate division (A) of this section;

(3) Refuse to bargain collectively with a public employer if the employee organization is recognized as the exclusive representative or certified as the exclusive representative of public employees in a bargaining unit;

(4) Call, institute, maintain, or conduct a boycott against any public employer, or picket any place of business of a public employer, on account of any jurisdictional work dispute;

(5) Induce or encourage any individual employed by any person to engage in a strike in violation of Chapter 4117. of the Revised Code or refusal to handle goods or perform services; or threaten, coerce, or restrain any person where an object thereof is to force or require any public employee to cease dealing or doing business with any other person, or force or require a public employer to recognize for representation purposes an employee organization not certified by the state employment relations board;

(6) Fail to fairly represent all public employees in a bargaining unit;

(7) Induce or encourage any individual in connection with a labor relations dispute to picket the residence or any place of private employment of any public official or representative of the public employer;

(8) Engage in any picketing, striking, or other concerted refusal to work without giving written notice to the public employer and to the state employment relations board not less than ten days prior to the action. The notice shall state the date and time that the action will commence and, once the notice is given, the parties may extend it by the written agreement of both.

(C) The determination by the board or any court that a public officer or employee has committed any of the acts prohibited by divisions (A) and (B) of this section shall not be made the basis of any charge for the removal from office or recall of the public officer or the suspension from or termination of employment of or disciplinary acts against an employee, nor shall the officer or employee be found subject to any suit for damages based on such a determination; however nothing in this division prevents any party to a collective bargaining agreement from seeking enforcement or damages for a violation thereof against the other party to the agreement.

(D) As to jurisdictional work disputes, the board shall hear and determine the dispute unless, within ten days after notice to the board by a party to the dispute that a dispute exists, the parties to the dispute submit to the board satisfactory evidence that they have adjusted, or agreed upon the method for the voluntary adjustment of, the dispute.

Effective Date: 04-01-1984

The amendment to this section by 129th General Assembly File No. 10, SB 5, § 1 was rejected by voters in the November, 2011 election.

4117.12 Board to investigate charge of violation.

(A) Whoever violates section 4117.11 of the Revised Code is guilty of an unfair labor practice remediable by the state employment relations board as specified in this section.

(B) When anyone files a charge with the board alleging that an unfair labor practice has been committed, the board or its designated agent shall investigate the charge. If the board has probable cause for believing that a violation has occurred, the board shall issue a complaint and shall conduct a hearing concerning the charge. The board shall cause the complaint to be served upon the charged party which shall contain a notice of the time at which the hearing on the complaint will be held either before the board, a board member, or an administrative law judge. The board may not issue a notice of hearing based upon any unfair labor practice occurring more than ninety days prior to the filing of the charge with the board, unless the person aggrieved thereby is prevented from filing the charge by reason of service in the armed forces, in which event the ninety-day period shall be computed from the day of the person's discharge. If the board dismisses a complaint as frivolous, it shall assess costs to the complainant pursuant to its standards governing such matters, and for that purpose, the board shall adopt a rule defining the standards by which the board will declare a complaint to be frivolous and the costs that will be assessed accordingly.

(1) The board, board member, or administrative law judge shall hold a hearing on the charge within ten days after service of the complaint. The board may amend a complaint, upon receipt of a notice from the charging party, at any time prior to the close of the hearing, and the charged party shall within ten days from receipt of the complaint or amendment to the complaint, file an answer to the complaint or amendment to the complaint. The charged party may file an answer to an original or amended complaint. The agents of the board and the person charged are parties and may appear or otherwise give evidence at the hearing. At the discretion of the board, board member, or administrative law judge, any interested party may intervene and present evidence at the hearing. The board, board member, or administrative law judge is not bound by the rules of evidence prevailing in the courts.

(2) A board member or administrative law judge who conducts the hearing shall reduce the evidence taken to writing and file it with the board. The board member or the administrative law judge may thereafter take further evidence or hear further argument if notice is given to all interested parties. The administrative law judge or board member shall issue to the parties a proposed decision, together with a recommended order and file it with the board. If the parties file no exceptions within twenty days after service thereof, the recommended order becomes the order of the board effective as therein prescribed. If the parties file exceptions to the proposed report, the board shall determine whether substantial issues have been raised. The board may rescind or modify the proposed order of the board member or administrative law judge; however, if the board determines that the exceptions do not raise substantial issues of fact or law, it may refuse to grant review, and the recommended order becomes effective as therein prescribed.

(3) If upon the preponderance of the evidence taken, the board believes that any person named in the complaint has engaged in any unfair labor practice, the board shall state its findings of fact and issue and cause to be served on the person an order requiring that the person cease and desist from these unfair labor practices, and take such affirmative action, including reinstatement of employees with or without back pay, as will effectuate the policies of Chapter 4117. of the Revised Code. If upon a preponderance of the evidence taken, the board believes that the person named in the complaint has not engaged in an unfair labor practice it shall state its findings of fact and issue an order dismissing the complaint.

(4) The board may order the public employer to reinstate the public employee and further may order either the public employer or the employee organization, depending on who was responsible for the discrimination suffered by the public employee, to make such payment of back pay to the public employee as the board determines. No order of the board shall require the reinstatement of any individual as an employee who has been suspended or discharged, or require the payment to the employee of any back pay, if the suspension or discharge was for just cause not related to rights provided in section 4117.03 of the Revised Code and the procedure contained in the collective bargaining agreement governing

suspension or discharge was followed. The order of the board may require the party against whom the order is issued to make periodic reports showing the extent to which the party has complied with the order.

(C) Whenever a complaint alleges that a person has engaged in an unfair labor practice and that the complainant will suffer substantial and irreparable injury if not granted temporary relief, the board may petition the court of common pleas for any county wherein the alleged unfair labor practice in question occurs, or wherein any person charged with the commission of any unfair labor practice resides or transacts business for appropriate injunctive relief, pending the final adjudication by the board with respect to the matter. Upon the filing of any petition, the court shall cause notice thereof to be served upon the parties, and thereupon has jurisdiction to grant the temporary relief or restraining order it considers just and proper.

(D) Until the record in a case is filed in a court, as specified in Chapter 4117. of the Revised Code, the board may at any time upon reasonable notice and in a manner it considers proper, modify or set aside, in whole or in part, any finding or order made or issued by it.

Amended by 128th General Assembly File No. 9, HB 1, § 101.01, eff. 7/17/2009.

Effective Date: 04-01-1984

The amendment to this section by 129th General Assembly File No. 10, SB 5, § 1 was rejected by voters in the November, 2011 election.

4117.13   Board or party may petition court of common pleas.

(A) The state employment relations board or the complaining party may petition the court of common pleas for any county wherein an unfair labor practice occurs, or wherein any person charged with the commission of any unfair labor practice resides or transacts business, for the enforcement of the order and for appropriate temporary relief or restraining order. The board shall certify and file in the court a transcript of the entire record in the proceeding, including the pleadings and evidence upon which the order was entered and the findings and order of the board. When the board petitions the court, the complaining party may intervene in the case as a matter of right. Upon the filing, the court shall cause notice thereof to be served upon the person charged with committing the unfair labor practice and thereupon has jurisdiction of the proceeding and the question determined therein. The court may grant the temporary relief or restraining order it deems just and proper, and make and enter upon the pleadings, evidence, and proceedings set forth in the transcript a decree enforcing, modifying, and enforcing as so modified, or setting aside in whole or in part the order of the board.

(B) The findings of the board as to the facts, if supported by substantial evidence, on the record as a whole, are conclusive. If either party applies to the court for leave to adduce additional evidence and shows to the satisfaction of the court that the additional evidence is material and that there exist reasonable grounds for the failure to adduce the evidence in the hearing before the board, its member or agent, the court may order the board, its member, or agent to take the additional evidence, and make it a part of the transcript. The board may modify its findings as to the facts, or make new findings, by reason of additional evidence so taken and filed, and it shall file the modified or new findings, which, if supported by the evidence, are conclusive and shall file its recommendations, if any, for the modifying or setting aside of its original order.

(C) The jurisdiction of the court is exclusive and its judgment and decree final, except that the same is subject to review on questions of law as in civil cases.

(D) Any person aggrieved by any final order of the board granting or denying, in whole or in part, the relief sought may appeal to the court of common pleas of any county where the unfair labor practice in question was alleged to have been engaged in, or where the person resides or transacts business, by filing in the court a notice of appeal setting forth the order appealed from and the grounds of appeal. The court shall cause a copy of the notice to be served forthwith upon the board. Within ten days after the court receives a notice of appeal, the board shall file in the court a transcript of the entire record in the proceeding, certified by the board, including the pleading and evidence upon which the order appealed from was entered.

The court has exclusive jurisdiction to grant the temporary relief or restraining order it considers proper, and to make and enter a decree enforcing, modifying, and enforcing as so modified, or setting aside in whole or in part the order of the board. The findings of the board as to the facts, if supported by substantial evidence on the record as a whole, are conclusive.

(E) The commencement of proceedings under division (A) or (D) of this section does not, unless specifically ordered by the court, operate as a stay of the board's order.

(F) Courts of common pleas shall hear appeals under Chapter 4117. of the Revised Code expeditiously presented and where good cause is shown give precedence to them over all other civil matters except earlier matters of the same character.

Effective Date: 04-01-1984

The amendment to this section by 129th General Assembly File No. 10, SB 5, § 1 was rejected by voters in the November, 2011 election.

4117.14 Settlement of dispute between exclusive representative and public employer — procedures.

(A) The procedures contained in this section govern the settlement of disputes between an exclusive representative and a public employer concerning the termination or modification of an existing collective bargaining agreement or negotiation of a successor agreement, or the negotiation of an initial collective bargaining agreement.

(B)

(1) In those cases where there exists a collective bargaining agreement, any public employer or exclusive representative desiring to terminate, modify, or negotiate a successor collective bargaining agreement shall:

(a) Serve written notice upon the other party of the proposed termination, modification, or successor agreement. The party must serve the notice not less than sixty days prior to the expiration date of the existing agreement or, in the event the existing collective bargaining agreement does not contain an expiration date, not less than sixty days prior to the time it is proposed to make the termination or modifications or to make effective a successor agreement.

(b) Offer to bargain collectively with the other party for the purpose of modifying or terminating any existing agreement or negotiating a successor agreement;

(c) Notify the state employment relations board of the offer by serving upon the board a copy of the written notice to the other party and a copy of the existing collective bargaining agreement.

(2) In the case of initial negotiations between a public employer and an exclusive representative, where a collective bargaining agreement has not been in effect between the parties, any party may serve notice upon the board and the other party setting forth the names and addresses of the parties and offering to meet, for a period of ninety days, with the other party for the purpose of negotiating a collective bargaining agreement.

If the settlement procedures specified in divisions (B), (C), and (D) of this section govern the parties, where those procedures refer to the expiration of a collective bargaining agreement, it means the expiration of the sixty-day period to negotiate a collective bargaining agreement referred to in this subdivision, or in the case of initial negotiations, it means the ninety day period referred to in this subdivision.

(3) The parties shall continue in full force and effect all the terms and conditions of any existing collective bargaining agreement, without resort to strike or lock-out, for a period of sixty days after the party gives notice or until the expiration date of the collective bargaining agreement, whichever occurs later, or for a period of ninety days where applicable.

(4) Upon receipt of the notice, the parties shall enter into collective bargaining.

(C) In the event the parties are unable to reach an agreement, they may submit, at any time prior to forty-five days before the expiration date of the collective bargaining agreement, the issues in dispute to any mutually agreed upon dispute settlement procedure which supersedes the procedures contained in this section.

(1) The procedures may include:

(a) Conventional arbitration of all unsettled issues;

(b) Arbitration confined to a choice between the last offer of each party to the agreement as a single package;

(c) Arbitration confined to a choice of the last offer of each party to the agreement on each issue submitted;

(d) The procedures described in division (C)(1)(a), (b), or (c) of this section and including among the choices for the arbitrator, the recommendations of the fact finder, if there are recommendations, either as a single package or on each issue submitted;

(e) Settlement by a citizens' conciliation council composed of three residents within the jurisdiction of the public employer. The public employer shall select one member and the exclusive representative shall select one member. The two members selected shall select the third member who shall chair the council. If the two members cannot agree upon a third member within five days after their appointments, the board shall appoint the third member. Once appointed, the council shall make a final settlement of the issues submitted to it pursuant to division (G) of this section.

(f) Any other dispute settlement procedure mutually agreed to by the parties.

(2) If, fifty days before the expiration date of the collective bargaining agreement, the parties are unable to reach an agreement, any party may request the state employment relations board to intervene. The request shall set forth the names and addresses of the parties, the issues involved, and, if applicable, the expiration date of any agreement.

The board shall intervene and investigate the dispute to determine whether the parties have engaged in collective bargaining.

If an impasse exists or forty-five days before the expiration date of the collective bargaining agreement if one exists, the board shall appoint a mediator to assist the parties in the collective bargaining process.

(3) Any time after the appointment of a mediator, either party may request the appointment of a fact-finding panel. Within fifteen days after receipt of a request for a fact-finding panel, the board shall appoint a fact-finding panel of not more than three members who have been selected by the parties in accordance with rules established by the board, from a list of qualified persons maintained by the board.

(a) The fact-finding panel shall, in accordance with rules and procedures established by the board that include the regulation of costs and expenses of fact-finding, gather facts and make recommendations for the resolution of the matter. The board shall by its rules require each party to specify in writing the unresolved issues and its position on each issue to the fact-finding panel. The fact-finding panel shall make final recommendations as to all the unresolved issues.

(b) The board may continue mediation, order the parties to engage in collective bargaining until the expiration date of the agreement, or both.

(4) The following guidelines apply to fact-finding:

(a) The fact-finding panel may establish times and place of hearings which shall be, where feasible, in the jurisdiction of the state.

(b) The fact-finding panel shall conduct the hearing pursuant to rules established by the board.

(c) Upon request of the fact-finding panel, the board shall issue subpoenas for hearings conducted by the panel.

(d) The fact-finding panel may administer oaths.

(e) The board shall prescribe guidelines for the fact-finding panel to follow in making findings. In making its recommendations, the fact-finding panel shall take into consideration the factors listed in divisions (G)(7)(a) to (f) of this section.

(f) The fact-finding panel may attempt mediation at any time during the fact-finding process. From the time of appointment until the fact-finding panel makes a final recommendation, it shall not discuss the recommendations for settlement of the dispute with parties other than the direct parties to the dispute.

(5) The fact-finding panel, acting by a majority of its members, shall transmit its findings of fact and recommendations on the unresolved issues to the public employer and employee organization involved and to the board no later than fourteen days after the appointment of the fact-finding panel, unless the parties mutually agree to an extension. The parties shall share the cost of the fact-finding panel in a manner agreed to by the parties.

(6)

(a) Not later than seven days after the findings and recommendations are sent, the legislative body, by a three-fifths vote of its total membership, and in the case of the public employee organization, the membership, by a three-fifths vote of the total membership, may reject the recommendations; if neither rejects the recommendations, the recommendations shall be deemed agreed upon as the final resolution of the issues submitted and a collective bargaining agreement shall be executed between the parties, including the fact-finding panel's recommendations, except as otherwise modified by the parties by mutual agreement. If either the legislative body or the public employee organization rejects the recommendations, the board shall publicize the findings of fact and recommendations of the fact-finding panel. The board shall adopt rules governing the procedures and methods for public employees to vote on the recommendations of the fact-finding panel.

(b) As used in division (C)(6)(a) of this section, "legislative body" means the controlling board when the state or any of its agencies, authorities, commissions, boards, or other branch of public employment is party to the fact-finding process.

(D) If the parties are unable to reach agreement within seven days after the publication of findings and recommendations from the fact-finding panel or the collective bargaining agreement, if one exists, has expired, then the:

(1) Public employees, who are members of a police or fire department, members of the state highway patrol, deputy sheriffs, dispatchers employed by a police, fire or sheriff's department or the state highway patrol or civilian dispatchers employed by a public employer other than a police, fire, or sheriff's department to dispatch police, fire, sheriff's department, or emergency medical or rescue personnel and units, an exclusive nurse's unit, employees of the state school for the deaf or the state school for the blind, employees of any public employee retirement system, corrections officers, guards at penal or mental institutions, special police officers appointed in accordance with sections 5119.14

and 5123.13 of the Revised Code, psychiatric attendants employed at mental health forensic facilities, youth leaders employed at juvenile correctional facilities, or members of a law enforcement security force that is established and maintained exclusively by a board of county commissioners and whose members are employed by that board, shall submit the matter to a final offer settlement procedure pursuant to a board order issued forthwith to the parties to settle by a conciliator selected by the parties. The parties shall request from the board a list of five qualified conciliators and the parties shall select a single conciliator from the list by alternate striking of names. If the parties cannot agree upon a conciliator within five days after the board order, the board shall on the sixth day after its order appoint a conciliator from a list of qualified persons maintained by the board or shall request a list of qualified conciliators from the American arbitration association and appoint therefrom.

(2) Public employees other than those listed in division (D)(1) of this section have the right to strike under Chapter 4117. of the Revised Code provided that the employee organization representing the employees has given a ten-day prior written notice of an intent to strike to the public employer and to the board, and further provided that the strike is for full, consecutive work days and the beginning date of the strike is at least ten work days after the ending date of the most recent prior strike involving the same bargaining unit; however, the board, at its discretion, may attempt mediation at any time.

(E) Nothing in this section shall be construed to prohibit the parties, at any time, from voluntarily agreeing to submit any or all of the issues in dispute to any other alternative dispute settlement procedure. An agreement or statutory requirement to arbitrate or to settle a dispute pursuant to a final offer settlement procedure and the award issued in accordance with the agreement or statutory requirement is enforceable in the same manner as specified in division (B) of section 4117.09 of the Revised Code.

(F) Nothing in this section shall be construed to prohibit a party from seeking enforcement of a collective bargaining agreement or a conciliator's award as specified in division (B) of section 4117.09 of the Revised Code.

(G) The following guidelines apply to final offer settlement proceedings under division (D)(1) of this section:

(1) The parties shall submit to final offer settlement those issues that are subject to collective bargaining as provided by section 4117.08 of the Revised Code and upon which the parties have not reached agreement and other matters mutually agreed to by the public employer and the exclusive representative; except that the conciliator may attempt mediation at any time.

(2) The conciliator shall hold a hearing within thirty days of the board's order to submit to a final offer settlement procedure, or as soon thereafter as is practicable.

(3) The conciliator shall conduct the hearing pursuant to rules developed by the board. The conciliator shall establish the hearing time and place, but it shall be, where feasible, within the jurisdiction of the state. Not later than five calendar days before the hearing, each of the parties shall submit to the conciliator, to the

opposing party, and to the board, a written report summarizing the unresolved issues, the party's final offer as to the issues, and the rationale for that position.

(4) Upon the request by the conciliator, the board shall issue subpoenas for the hearing.

(5) The conciliator may administer oaths.

(6) The conciliator shall hear testimony from the parties and provide for a written record to be made of all statements at the hearing. The board shall submit for inclusion in the record and for consideration by the conciliator the written report and recommendation of the fact-finders.

(7) After hearing, the conciliator shall resolve the dispute between the parties by selecting, on an issue-by-issue basis, from between each of the party's final settlement offers, taking into consideration the following:

(a) Past collectively bargained agreements, if any, between the parties;

(b) Comparison of the issues submitted to final offer settlement relative to the employees in the bargaining unit involved with those issues related to other public and private employees doing comparable work, giving consideration to factors peculiar to the area and classification involved;

(c) The interests and welfare of the public, the ability of the public employer to finance and administer the issues proposed, and the effect of the adjustments on the normal standard of public service;

(d) The lawful authority of the public employer;

(e) The stipulations of the parties;

(f) Such other factors, not confined to those listed in this section, which are normally or traditionally taken into consideration in the determination of the issues submitted to final offer settlement through voluntary collective bargaining, mediation, fact-finding, or other impasse resolution procedures in the public service or in private employment.

(8) Final offer settlement awards made under Chapter 4117. of the Revised Code are subject to Chapter 2711. of the Revised Code.

(9) If more than one conciliator is used, the determination must be by majority vote.

(10) The conciliator shall make written findings of fact and promulgate a written opinion and order upon the issues presented to the conciliator, and upon the record made before the conciliator and shall mail or otherwise deliver a true copy thereof to the parties and the board.

(11) Increases in rates of compensation and other matters with cost implications awarded by the conciliator may be effective only at the start of the fiscal year next commencing after the date of the final offer settlement award; provided that if a new fiscal year has commenced since the issuance of the board order to submit to a final offer settlement procedure, the awarded increases may be retroactive to the commencement of the new fiscal year. The parties may, at any

time, amend or modify a conciliator's award or order by mutual agreement.

(12) The parties shall bear equally the cost of the final offer settlement procedure.

(13) Conciliators appointed pursuant to this section shall be residents of the state.

(H) All final offer settlement awards and orders of the conciliator made pursuant to Chapter 4117. of the Revised Code are subject to review by the court of common pleas having jurisdiction over the public employer as provided in Chapter 2711. of the Revised Code. If the public employer is located in more than one court of common pleas district, the court of common pleas in which the principal office of the chief executive is located has jurisdiction.

(I) The issuance of a final offer settlement award constitutes a binding mandate to the public employer and the exclusive representative to take whatever actions are necessary to implement the award.

Effective Date: 06-26-2003; 01-27-2005; 2008 HB562 09-23-2008

The amendment to this section by 129th General Assembly File No. 10, SB 5, § 1 was rejected by voters in the November, 2011 election.

4117.15   Strike — injunction.

(A) Whenever a strike by members of a police or fire department, members of the state highway patrol, deputy sheriffs, dispatchers employed by a police, fire or sheriff's department or the state highway patrol or civilian dispatchers employed by a public employer other than a police, fire, or sheriff's department to dispatch police, fire, sheriff's department, or emergency medical or rescue personnel and units, an exclusive nurse's unit, employees of the state school for the deaf or the state school for the blind, employees of any public employee retirement system, correction officers, guards at penal or mental institutions, or special police officers appointed in accordance with sections 5119.14 and 5123.13 of the Revised Code, psychiatric attendants employed at mental health forensic facilities, youth leaders employed at juvenile correctional facilities, or members of a law enforcement security force that is established and maintained exclusively by a board of county commissioners and whose members are employed by that board, a strike by other public employees during the pendency of the settlement procedures set forth in section 4117.14 of the Revised Code, or a strike during the term or extended term of a collective bargaining agreement occurs, the public employer may seek an injunction against the strike in the court of common pleas of the county in which the strike is located.

(B) An unfair labor practice by a public employer is not a defense to the injunction proceeding noted in division (A) of this section. Allegations of unfair labor practices during the settlement procedures set forth in section 4117.14 of the Revised Code shall receive priority by the state employment relations board.

(C) No public employee is entitled to pay or compensation from the public employer for the period engaged in any strike.

Effective Date: 04-01-1984; 2008 HB562 09-23-2008

The amendment to this section by 129th General Assembly File No. 10, SB 5, § 1 was rejected by voters in the November, 2011 election.

4117.16   Temporary restraining order enjoining strike.

(A) Whenever the public employer believes that a lawful strike creates clear and present danger to the health or safety of the public, the public employer may petition the court of common pleas having jurisdiction over the parties to issue a temporary restraining order enjoining the strike. If the court finds probable cause to believe that the strike may be a clear and present danger to the public health or safety, it has jurisdiction to issue a temporary restraining order, not to exceed seventy-two hours, enjoining the strike.

Should a court issue a temporary restraining order, the public employer shall immediately request authorization of the state employment relations board to enjoin the strike beyond the effective period of the temporary restraining order. The board shall determine within the effective period of the temporary restraining order whether the strike creates a clear and present danger to the health or safety of the public.

If the board finds that a clear and present danger exists, the common pleas court which issued the temporary restraining order has jurisdiction to issue orders to further enjoin the strike. However, the court shall make provisions in any injunction or other order issued beyond the temporary restraining order for the automatic termination of the injunction or other order at the end of sixty days following the end of the temporary restraining order or when an agreement is reached, whichever occurs first. Thereafter, no court has jurisdiction to issue any further injunction or other orders pursuant to this section. The order of the court is appealable as provided in the Appellate Rules.

(B) Whenever a court of common pleas has issued an order, other than a temporary restraining order, under division (A) of this section enjoining acts or practices which create a clear and present danger to the public health or safety, the parties to the labor dispute giving rise to the order shall engage in collective bargaining for a period of sixty days from the date of the order or until agreement is reached, whichever occurs first. The parties shall collectively bargain with the assistance of a mediator appointed by the board. The mediator, at his discretion, may require that the parties collectively bargain in public or in private. At any time after there has been forty-five days of collective bargaining and no agreement has been reached, the mediator may make public a report on the current position of the parties to the dispute and the efforts which have been made for settlement. The report shall include a statement by each party of its position and a statement of the employee organization's and public employer's offers of settlement.

Effective Date: 04-01-1984

The repeal of this section by 129th General Assembly File No. 10, SB 5, § 2 was rejected by voters in the November, 2011 election.

4117.17   Board proceedings are public records.

Formal charges, petitions, complaints, orders, evidence, fact-finding recommendations, and other proceedings instituted by the state employment relations board under Chapter 4117. of the Revised Code are public records and available for inspection or copying subject to rules made by the board. All hearings on complaints or petitions pursuant to Chapter 4117. of the Revised Code are open to the public.

Effective Date: 04-01-1984

4117.18 Prohibited acts.

(A) No person shall purposely refuse to obey an order issued by a court of competent jurisdiction under Chapter 4117. of the Revised Code.

(B) No person shall purposely refuse to obey a lawful order of the state employment relations board, nor shall any person prevent or attempt to prevent any member of the board or any agent of the board from performing his lawful duties.

(C) No public employee shall engage in any unauthorized strike.

Effective Date: 09-21-1995

The amendment to this section by 129th General Assembly File No. 10, SB 5, § 1 was rejected by voters in the November, 2011 election.

4117.19 Employee organization reports.

(A) Every employee organization that is certified or recognized as a representative of public employees under this chapter shall file with the state employment relations board a registration report that is signed by its president or other appropriate officer. The report shall be in a form prescribed by the board and accompanied by two copies of the employee organization's constitution and bylaws. The board shall accept a filing by a statewide, national, or international employee organization of its constitution and bylaws in lieu of a filing of the documents by each subordinate organization. The exclusive representative or other employee organization originally filing its constitution and bylaws shall report, promptly, to the board all changes or amendments to its constitution and bylaws.

(B) Every employee organization shall file with the board an annual report. The report shall be in a form prescribed by the board and shall contain the following information:

(1) The names and addresses of the organization, any parent organization or organizations with which it is affiliated, and all organization-wide officers;

(2) The name and address of its local agent for service of process;

(3) A general description of the public employees the organization represents or seeks to represent;

(4) The amounts of the initiation fee and monthly dues members must pay;

(5) A pledge, in a form prescribed by the board, that the organization will comply with the laws of the state and that it will accept members without regard to age, race, color, sex, creed, religion, ancestry, national origin, disability as defined in section 4112.01 of the Revised Code, military status as defined in that section, or physical disability as provided by law:

(6) A financial report.

(C) The constitution or bylaws of every employee organization shall do all of the following:

(1) Require that the organization keep accurate accounts of all income and expenses, prepare an annual financial report, keep open for inspection by any member of the organization its accounts, and make loans to officers and agents only on terms and conditions available to all members;

(2) Prohibit business or financial interests of its officers and agents, their spouses, minor children, parents, or otherwise, in conflict with the fiduciary obligation of such persons to the organization;

(3) When specifically requested by the board, require every official who is designated as a fiscal officer of an employee organization and who is responsible for funds or other property of the organization or trust in which an organization is interested, or a subsidiary organization be bonded with the amount, scope, and form of the bond determined by the board;

(4) Require periodic elections of officers by secret ballot subject to recognized safeguards concerning the equal right of all members to nominate, seek office, and vote in the elections, the right of individual members to participate in the affairs of the organization, and fair and equitable procedures in disciplinary actions.

(D) The board shall prescribe rules necessary to govern the establishment and reporting of trusteeships over employee organizations. The establishment of trusteeships is permissible only if the constitution or bylaws of the organization set forth reasonable procedures.

(E) The board may withhold certification of an employee organization that willfully refuses to register or file an annual report or that willfully refuses to comply with other provisions of this section. The board may revoke a certification of an employee organization for willfully failing to comply with this section. The board may enforce the prohibitions contained in this section by petitioning the court of common pleas of the county in which the violation occurs for an injunction. Persons complaining of a violation of this section shall file the complaint with the board.

(F) Upon the written request to the board of any member of a certified employee organization and where the board determines the necessity for an audit, the board may require the employee organization to provide a certified audit of its financial records.

(G) Any employee organization subject to the "Labor-Management Reporting and Disclosure Act of 1959," 73 Stat. 519, 29 U.S.C.A., 401, as amended, may file copies with the board of all reports it is required to file under that act in lieu of compliance with all parts of this section other than division (A) of this section. The board shall accept a filing by a statewide, national, or international employee organization of its reports in lieu of a filing of such reports by each subordinate organization.

Effective Date: 03-17-2000; 2007 HB372 03-24-2008

4117.20   Prohibiting conflict of interest in bargaining.

(A) No person who is a member of the same local, state, national, or international organization as the employee organization with which the public employer is bargaining or who has an interest in the outcome of the bargaining, which interest is in conflict with the interest of the public employer, shall participate on behalf of the public employer in the collective bargaining process except that the person may, where entitled, vote on the ratification of an agreement.

(B) The public employer shall immediately remove from his role, if any, in the collective bargaining negotiations or in any matter in connection with negotiations any person who violates division (A) of this section.

Effective Date: 04-01-1984

The amendment to this section by 129th General Assembly File No. 10, SB 5, § 1 was rejected by voters in the November, 2011 election.

4117.21   Collective bargaining meetings private.

Collective bargaining meetings between public employers and employee organizations are private, and are not subject to section 121.22 of the Revised Code.

Effective Date: 04-01-1984

The amendment to this section by 129th General Assembly File No. 10, SB 5, § 1 was rejected by voters in the November, 2011 election.

4117.22   Chapter liberally construed.

Chapter 4117. of the Revised Code shall be construed liberally for the accomplishment of the purpose of promoting orderly and constructive relationships between all public employers and their employees.

Effective Date: 04-01-1984

The repeal of this section by 129th General Assembly File No. 10, SB 5, § 2 was rejected by voters in the November, 2011 election.

4117.23   Unauthorized strikes.

(A) In the case of a strike that is not authorized in accordance with this chapter, the public employer may notify the state employment relations board of the strike and request the board to determine whether the strike is authorized under Chapter 4117. of the Revised Code. The board shall make its decision within seventy-two hours of receiving the request from the public employer.

(B) If the board determines that the strike is not authorized then the public employer:

(1) May remove or suspend those employees who one day after notification by the public employer of the board decision that a strike is not authorized continue to engage in the nonauthorized strike; and

(2) If the employee is appointed or reappointed, employed, or reemployed, as a public employee, within the same appointing authority, may impose the following conditions:

(a) The employee's compensation shall in no event exceed that received by him immediately prior to the time of the violation.

(b) The employee's compensation is not increased until after the expiration of one year from the appointment or reappointment, employment, or reemployment.

(3) Shall deduct from each striking employee's wages, if the board also determines that the public employer did not provoke the strike, the equivalent of two days' wages for each day the employee remains on strike commencing one day after receiving the notice called for in division (B)(1) of this section. The employer shall give the employee credit for wages not paid after that point in time due to the employee's absence from his place of employment because he is on strike.

Any penalty that is imposed upon the employee, except for the penalty imposed under division (B)(3) of this section, may be appealed to the board. The board may modify, suspend, or reverse the penalty imposed by the public employer, if the board does not find that the penalties are appropriate to the situation; the imposition of a penalty is appealable to the court.

Notwithstanding the provision in this section that authorizes certain penalties to commence one day after a public employee is notified that the board has determined the employee is engaged in an unauthorized strike, the board may authorize the public employer, if the public employer requests it, to impose the penalties contained in this section retroactive to the date the unauthorized strike commences.

Effective Date: 04-01-1984

The repeal of this section by 129th General Assembly File No. 10, SB 5, § 2 was rejected by voters in the November, 2011 election.

4117.24 Training and publications fund.

(A) The training, publications, and grants fund is hereby created in the state treasury. The state employment relations board shall deposit into the training, publications, and grants fund all moneys received from the following sources:

(1) Payments received by the state employment relations board for copies of documents, rulebooks, and other publications;

(2) Fees received from seminar participants;

(3) Receipts from the sale of clearinghouse data;

(4) Moneys received from grants, donations, awards, bequests, gifts, reimbursements, and similar funds;

(5) Reimbursement received for professional services and expenses related to professional services;

(6) Funds received to support the development of labor relations services and programs;

(7) Moneys received by the state personnel board of review pursuant to division (C) of section 124.03 of the Revised Code.

(B) The state employment relations board shall use all moneys deposited into the training, publications, and grants fund to defray all of the following:

(1) The costs of furnishing and making available copies of documents, rulebooks, and other publications;

(2) The costs of planning, organizing, and conducting training seminars;

(3) The costs associated with grant projects, innovative labor-management cooperation programs, research projects related to these grants and programs, and the advancement in professionalism of public sector relations;

(4) The professional development of state employment relations board employees;

(5) The costs of compiling clearinghouse data;

(6) The cost of producing the administrative record of the state personnel board of review.

The state employment relations board may seek, solicit, apply for, receive, and accept grants, gifts, and contributions of money, property, labor, and other things of value to be held for, used for, and applied to only the purpose for which the grants, gifts, and contributions are made, from individuals, private and public corporations, the United States or any agency thereof, the state or any agency thereof, and any political subdivision of the state, and may enter into any contract with any such public or private source in connection therewith to be held for, used for, and applied to only the purposes for which such grants are made and contracts are entered into, all subject to and in accordance with the purposes of this chapter. Any money received from the grants, gifts, contributions, or contracts shall be deposited into the training, publications, and grants fund.

Amended by 128th General Assembly File No. 9, HB 1, § 101.01, eff. 7/17/2009.

Effective Date: 06-30-1999; 07-01-2005

EXAMPLE OF A REMEDIAL NOTICE

Excerpted from
Parts Depot, Inc. and Union of Needletrades
332 N.L.R.B. 670, 731–32 (2000)
The National Labor Relations Board

NOTICE TO EMPLOYEES

POSTED BY ORDER OF THE NATIONAL LABOR RELATIONS BOARD

An Agency of the United States Government

The National Labor Relations Board has found that we violated the National Labor Relations Act and has ordered us to post and abide by this notice.

Section 7 of the Act gives employees these rights.
To organize
To form, join, or assist any union
To bargain collectively through representatives of their own choice
To act together for other mutual aid or protection
To choose not to engage in any of these protected concerted activities.

WE WILL NOT grant you new benefits, issue you warnings, restrict your movements within the facility, prohibit your waiting in the facility for other employees, give you unfavorable job performance evaluations, lay you off, or otherwise discriminate against any of you for supporting Union of Needletrades, Industrial and Textile Employees, AFL-CIO, CLC (UNITE), (the Union) or any other union.

WE WILL NOT coercively interrogate any of you about union support or union activities.

WE WILL NOT offer you improved benefits for the purpose of dissuading you from supporting the Union.

WE WILL NOT threaten you with unspecified reprisals in order to dissuade you from supporting the Union.

WE WILL NOT unilaterally grant pay raises to bargaining unit employees without first consulting with the Union and offering the Union the opportunity to bargain over the decision and the effects of such pay increases.

WE WILL NOT unilaterally lay off bargaining unit employees for economic reasons without first consulting with the Union and offering the Union the opportunity to bargain over the decision and the effects of such layoffs.

WE WILL NOT in any like or related manner interfere with, restrain, or coerce you in the exercise of the rights guaranteed you by Section 7 of the Act.

WE WILL recognize and, on request, bargain with the Union as the exclusive representative of the employees in the following appropriate unit concerning terms and conditions of employment and, if an understanding is reached, embody the understanding in a signed agreement:

All warehouse employees, customer service employees, truck dispatcher, and drivers employed by Parts Depot, Inc. at its Miami and Ft. Lauderdale, Florida warehouses, excluding office clericals, technical employees, professional employees, supervisors, and guards as defined by the Act.

WE WILL, within 14 days from the date of the Board's Order, offer Vivian M. Fortin full reinstatement to the former job in phone sales which we would have given her absent the discrimination against her or, if that job no longer exists, reinstatement to a substantially equivalent position, without prejudice to her seniority or any other rights or privileges previously enjoyed.

WE WILL make whole Vivian M. Fortin for any loss of earnings and other benefits suffered as a result of the discrimination against her, in the manner set forth in the remedy section of the decision.

WE WILL, within 14 days from the date of the Board's Order, remove from our files any reference to the unlawful warnings which we issued to Vivian M. Fortin in June 1994, to the unlawful job performance evaluation which we gave to her on August 3, 1994, and to her unlawful layoff of October 27, 1994, and mark our records, including her personnel file, to show that Vivian M. Fortin is deemed to have received, on her August 1994 performance evaluation, and overall rating of 4, and within 3 days thereafter WE WILL notify Vivian M. Fortin in writing that this has been done and that such discriminatory actions will not be used against her in any way.

WE WILL, on request, bargain with the Union concerning the decisions to lay off bargaining unit employees effective August 11, 1994, and again on October 27, 1994, and the effects of those decisions.

WE WILL, within 14 days from the date of the Board's Order, offer the employees named below, laid off effective August 11, 1994, full reinstatement to their former jobs or, if those jobs no longer exist, to substantially equivalent positions, without prejudice to their seniority or any other rights or privileges previously enjoyed:

Carlos Boufartiguez	Isabel Martinez
Ronald Casco	Aundrai McGregor
Crystal Davis	Chester Umana
Jean-Claude Demosthene	Angela (Lampin) Wilson
Enrique Flores	Jaan Wilson
Ronaldo Hernandez	Altonia Wright

WE WILL, within 14 days from the date of the Board's Order, offer the employees named below, laid off effective October 27, 1994, full reinstatement to their former jobs or, if those jobs no longer exist, to substantially equivalent positions, without prejudice to their seniority or any other rights or privileges previously enjoyed:

Vivian M. Fortin	Annia Vigos

WE WILL make whole the employees named above, laid off effective August 11 and October 27, 1994, for any loss of earnings and other benefits suffered as a result of their unilateral layoffs, in the manner set forth in the remedy section of the decision.

CHARGE AGAINST EMPLOYER

https://www.nlrb.gov/sites/default/files/attachments/basic-page/node-3040/nlrbform501.pdf

---

Please Review the Following
Important Information
Before Filling Out a Charge Form!

- Please call an Information Officer in the Regional Office nearest you for assistance in filing a charge. The Information Officer will be happy to answer your questions about the charge form or to draft the charge on your behalf. Seeking assistance from an Information Officer may help you to avoid having the processing of your charge delayed or your charge dismissed because of mistakes made in completing the form.

- Please be advised that not every workplace action that you may view as unfair constitutes an unfair labor practice within the jurisdiction of the National Labor Relations Act (NLRA). Please click on the Help Desk button for more information on matters covered by the NLRA.

- The section of the charge form called, "Basis of Charge," seeks only a brief description of the alleged unfair labor practice. You should **NOT** include a detailed recounting of the evidence in support of the charge or a list of the names and telephone numbers of witnesses.

- After completing the charge form, be sure to sign and date the charge and mail or deliver the completed form to the appropriate Regional Office.

- A charge should be filed with the Regional Office which has jurisdiction over the geographic area of the United States where the unfair labor practice occurred. For example, an unfair labor practice charge alleging that an employer unlawfully discharged an employee would usually be filed with the Regional Office having jurisdiction over the worksite where the employee was employed prior to his/her discharge. An Information Officer will be pleased to assist you in locating the appropriate Regional Office in which to file your charge.

- The NLRB's Rules and Regulations state that it is the responsibility of the individual, employer or union filing a charge to timely and properly serve a copy of the charge on the person, employer or union against whom such charge is made.

- By statute, only charges filed and served within **six (6) months** of the date of the event or conduct, which is the subject of that charge, will be processed by the NLRB.

FORM EXEMPT UNDER 44 U.S.C 3512

INTERNET
FORM NLRB-501
(2-08)

UNITED STATES OF AMERICA
NATIONAL LABOR RELATIONS BOARD
CHARGE AGAINST EMPLOYER

DO NOT WRITE IN THIS SPACE

Case | Date Filed

INSTRUCTIONS:
File an original with NLRB Regional Director for the region in which the alleged unfair labor practice occurred or is occurring.

1. EMPLOYER AGAINST WHOM CHARGE IS BROUGHT

a. Name of Employer

b. Tel. No.

c. Cell No.

d. Address (Street, city, state, and ZIP code)

e. Employer Representative

f. Fax No.

g. e-Mail

h. Number of workers employed

i. Type of Establishment (factory, mine, wholesaler, etc.)

j. Identify principal product or service

k. The above-named employer has engaged in and is engaging in unfair labor practices within the meaning of section 8(a), subsections (1) and (list subsections) _____ of the National Labor Relations Act, and these unfair labor practices are practices affecting commerce within the meaning of the Act, or these unfair labor practices are unfair practices affecting commerce within the meaning of the Act and the Postal Reorganization Act.

2. Basis of the Charge (set forth a clear and concise statement of the facts constituting the alleged unfair labor practices)

3. Full name of party filing charge (if labor organization, give full name, including local name and number)

4a. Address (Street and number, city, state, and ZIP code)

4b. Tel. No.

4c. Cell No.

4d. Fax No.

4e. e-Mail

5. Full name of national or international labor organization of which it is an affiliate or constituent unit (to be filled in when charge is filed by a labor organization)

6. DECLARATION
I declare that I have read the above charge and that the statements are true to the best of my knowledge and belief.

By _____
(signature of representative or person making charge)   (Print/type name and title or office, if any)

Address _____   (date)

Tel. No.

Office, if any, Cell No.

Fax No.

e-Mail

WILLFUL FALSE STATEMENTS ON THIS CHARGE CAN BE PUNISHED BY FINE AND IMPRISONMENT (U.S. CODE, TITLE 18, SECTION 1001)
PRIVACY ACT STATEMENT

SAMPLE COLLECTIVE BARGAINING AGREEMENT

ARTICLE I
RECOGNITION

SEC. 1. The Company recognizes the Union as the exclusive bargaining agent for its employees, as defined herein, with respect to rates of pay, wages, hours of employment and conditions of employment. For the purpose of this Agreement the term "employee" shall include all hourly paid employees in the Company plants, but excluding Shift Superintendents, Assistant Superintendents, General Supervisor, Supervisor, Time Study Workers, Timekeepers, Plant Protection Workers and Salaried Employees.

SEC. 2. It shall be a condition of employment that all employees of the Employer covered by this Agreement who are members of the Union in good standing on the effective date of this Agreement shall remain members in good standing and those who are not members on the effective date of this Agreement shall, on and after the thirtieth day following the effective date of this Agreement, become and remain members in good standing in the Union. It shall also be a condition of employment that all employees covered by this Agreement and hired on or after its effective date shall, on and after the thirtieth day following the beginning of such employment, become and remain members in good standing in the Union. To satisfy the membership obligations imposed by this provision, bargaining unit personnel need only tender to the Union the periodic Union dues required of all members. Nonmembers who object to the Union's expenditure of periodic dues money for political or ideological purposes unrelated to collective bargaining or the administration of this Agreement, may notify the Union in writing of their objection and request a pro rata reduction in their periodic dues payment in direct proportion to the amount of money being expended for such unrelated purposes.

SEC. 3. The Union agrees that the functions of management are vested exclusively in the Company except as modified by the specific provisions of this Agreement. The Union, through its officers or members, will not interfere in the rights of the management in the matter of hiring, transfer, or promotion of employees from one department to another or within departments and in the general management of the plant insofar as the rights of the Union as defined in this Agreement are not affected adversely.

SEC. 4. The Union recognizes that the employer must be in a strong market position, which means it must produce efficiently. The Union, through its bargaining agency assumes responsibility for cooperating in the attainment of these goals. The Union therefore agrees that it will cooperate with the employer and support its efforts to assure a fair day's work on the part of its members. It further agrees that it will support the employer in its efforts to improve production; eliminate waste; conserve materials and supplies, improve the quality of workmanship; and strengthen good will between the employer and the employees.

ARTICLE II
DUES COLLECTION

SEC. 1. The Company will deduct from the pay of each employee covered by this Agreement who authorizes the Company to do so, all periodic Union dues, and the initiation fees uniformly required as a condition of acquiring or retaining membership. Such authorization to the Company must be in writing, signed by the employee and delivered to the Payroll Department.

(a) All such deductions shall be made during the first pay period of each calendar month.

(b) All sums deducted shall be remitted to the Financial Secretary of Local 157 not later than the 25th day of the calendar month in which such deductions are made.

(c) The Company and the Union shall work out a mutually satisfactory arrangement by which the Company will furnish the Financial Secretary of the Union and the Chief Steward of the unit monthly a record of those from whom deductions have been made, together with the amount of each deduction.

SEC. 2. The Company will also deduct from each employee covered by this Agreement, who authorizes the Company to do so, contributions in the amount of Five Dollars ($5.00) to the Shop Sickness and Flower Fund. The Chief Steward shall furnish the Payroll Department of the company, a list of all employees who are making contributions. The Company will give the Chief Steward a check for the amount so certified which shall be used by the unit for the Flower and welfare Fund.

ARTICLE III
REPRESENTATION

SEC. 1.

(a) There shall be one Committee person elected for each shift in operation at each plant. (1) The Committeeperson elected for the Day Shift at Plant No. 1 shall serve as the Chief Steward.

(b) There shall be one Steward for each shift in operation at each plant.

(c) There shall be a Steward representing the Truck Drivers and a Steward representing the Maintenance employees.

SEC. 2. The employees of the Company shall be represented by a Shop Committee as outlined in subsections (a) and (b).

(a) For the purpose of making agreements over and above the normal contract language during the term of the contract, and for negotiations of the new contract, the Shop Committee shall have the following make up:

(1) Six (6) committeepersons (one from each shift from both plants; one of this number to be the Chief Steward).

(2) The Truck Driver's Steward and the Maintenance Steward shall serve on

the Shop Committee when matters directly affecting their respective departments are involved.

(b) For the purpose of Steps 3, 4 and 5 of the grievance procedure, the Plant Grievance Committee shall be composed in the following manner:

(1) Plant I — Chief Steward, Afternoon committeeperson, Midnight Committeeperson.

(2) Plant II — Chief Steward, Day committeeperson, Afternoon Committeeperson, Midnight Committeeperson.

(3) At either plant, the Truck Drivers of Maintenance Steward when he wrote the grievance.

SEC. 3. A written list of members of the Committee and Stewards shall be furnished the Company and any changes shall be given in writing immediately after such change is made.

SEC. 4. The Union has a right to designate alternates and such alternates shall be recognized by the Company, during the absence of the regular Committeeperson or Steward.

SEC. 5. No official of the Union, including members of the Bargaining Committee and Stewards, shall assume any supervisory authority, nor advise nor direct employees to disregard the instructions of supervision unless those instructions will impose a clear hazard to the employee's health and safety.

SEC. 6. Stewards and Committeepersons, including the Chief Steward, shall notify their Shift Superintendent before leaving their department on Union business and shall punch their Labor Relations time cards. When they have completed their grievance duties, they shall notify their Shift Superintendent and punch out their Labor Relations cards before resuming work.

SEC. 7. Each Steward and Committeeperson shall be allowed all necessary time on his own shift without loss of pay for performing his duties in the grievance procedure and for all other meetings with management. When meetings with management at Steps 3, 4 and 5 of the grievance procedure require a Steward or Committeeperson other than the day shift man to spend time outside of his own shift, the Steward or Committeeperson shall receive compensating time off of his own shift at the next opportunity for time required.

ARTICLE IV
GRIEVANCES

SEC. 1. All grievances shall be handled in accordance with the following procedure:

(a) Step One: Any employee along with his/her steward having a grievance shall promptly take the matter up with his/her supervisor or shift superintendent. The steward shall be allowed to consult with the Chief Steward if necessary. If the employee's supervisor or superintendent is unable to adjust the matter immediately, then the grievance shall be reduced to writing by the steward which shall state the section of the contract alleged to have been violated. The supervisor or shift superintendent shall have two working days to give his answer in writing stating his reasons.

(b) Step Two: If not adjusted at Step One, the grievance shall be referred to the Chief Steward and the steward involved, who shall take it up within three working days with a representative of the Company, superior to the shift superintendent or supervisor, along with the shift superintendent or supervisor. This Company official shall have three (3) working days to answer the grievance in writing.

(c) Step Three: If not adjusted at Step Two, the grievance shall be referred to the plant grievance committee at the plant where the grievance arose, who shall take it up with the management within three (3) working days. Management shall have three (3) working days to answer the grievance in writing after such meeting.

(d) Step Four: If not adjusted at Step Three, by management, either party may within five (5) working days request a second meeting with outside representatives present for either party. A written answer shall be given to the moving arty within five (5) working days of this meeting.

(e) Step Five: Arbitration. If the grievance has not been satisfactorily settled between the plant grievance committee and management, either party may refer the matter to arbitration before the Umpire selected by the parties. The parties shall select an Umpire to act as arbitrator in all cases which reach he arbitration step of the grievance procedure. The Umpire shall serve so long as he/she continues to be acceptable to both parties. In the event the parties are unable to agree on selection of a permanent umpire, an arbitrator shall be selected in accordance with the rules of the American Arbitration Association. The fee of the Umpire and any other expenses incidental to the arbitration procedure shall be borne equally by both parties. The decision of the arbitrator shall be final and binding on both parties. The Umpire shall have no power to add to, subtract from, or modify any of the terms of this Agreement or any Agreement made supplemental hereto, nor to establish or change any job rate, nor to rule on any dispute relating to production standards, but shall refer any such case back to the parties without decision. The Union has the right to strike on these items after exhausting the grievance procedure through Step Four. In the event such strike action is taken under this provision, all other terms and conditions of this Agreement shall remain in full force and effect. All other items are subject to arbitration.

SEC. 2. It is the intent of the parties hereto that the procedure set forth herein shall serve as a means for the peaceful settlement of all disputes that may arise between them. Accordingly, if any dispute should arise between Company and any of its employees or the Union, there shall be no interruption of operations by the Company or by the Union or any employees.

SEC. 3. Neither the International Union, the Local Union, nor any of their officers, agents or representatives shall be liable to the Company in any action at law for damages arising out of any interruption of the Company's operations which is in violation of any provision of this Agreement if such interruption is neither instigated, authorized, sanctioned, ratified nor supported by the International or the Local Union, provided that they immediately take steps to remedy the condition. The exclusive remedy of the Company for such a violation shall be that any employee who instigates any such violation shall be subject to immediate discharge or discipline by the Company, and any employee who participates in such action may be disciplined.

SEC. 4. Any grievance will be automatically granted if the Company fails to give a disposition within the specified time limit in that step of the grievance procedure. Any grievance not advanced to the next step by the Union within the time limit specified in that step shall be deemed abandoned. Time limits may be extended by the Union and the Company in writing; then the new date shall prevail.

SEC. 5. Complaints regarding unjust and discriminatory dismissals must be filed within three (3) working days of the dismissals and the Company agrees to render a decision within two (2) working days of the receipt of such complaint. If such a complaint is denied, it shall be handled as a grievance under the grievance procedure.

SEC. 6. Any employee whose employment is found to have been unjustly terminated will be reinstated to work of a similar class at the same rate of pay and reimbursed at his regular rate of pay for lost time, subject to the limitations of this Article, except as the Umpire may have ruled differently.

SEC. 7. No claims, including claims for back wages, by an employee covered by this Agreement, or by the Union, against the Company shall be valid for a period prior to the date the grievance was first filed in writing, unless the circumstances of the case made it impossible for the employee, or for the Union as the case may be, to know that he, or the Union, had grounds for such a claim prior to that date, in which case the claim shall be limited retroactively to a period of sixty (60) days prior to the date the claim was first filed in writing.

SEC. 8. An agreement reached between the management and the shop committee is binding on all union members except where the International Union, or the Local 157 has to approve same.

SEC. 9. Disputes growing out of the interpretation of this Agreement and grievances which management may have shall follow the grievance procedure herein-above set forth, except that such grievances may be initiated at the shop committee level of this grievance procedure.

ARTICLE V
EMPLOYMENT PRACTICES AND DISCIPLINE

SEC. 1. The provisions of this Agreement shall apply to all employees covered by this Agreement without discrimination on account of age, race, color, national origin, marital status, gender, disability, or creed.

SEC. 2. No employee shall be disciplined or discharged except for just cause, unless in case of reorganization or layoff. "Just cause" shall be defined to include the concept of progressive discipline (such as verbal and written reprimands and the possibility of suspension without pay). Progressive discipline shall not be applied when the nature of the offense requires immediate suspension or discharge.

SEC. 3. The employee will be tendered a copy of any warning, reprimand, suspension or disciplinary layoff entered on his/her personal record within three (3) days of the action taken. In imposing discipline on a current charge, the Company will not take into account any prior infractions which occurred more than three years previously.

ARTICLE VI
SENIORITY

SEC. 1. It is agreed that employees for the purpose of layoff and recall, and for job, shift, and plant preference as herein provided, shall have plant-wide seniority. Employees may be transferred in accordance with the provisions of this Article from one department to another without affecting their seniority.

SEC. 2. Employees shall have their seniority listed on a plant-wide basis within their department and any transfer from that department to another shall be based on such seniority listing. The Company shall keep a correct seniority list of all employees having seniority and a list showing classifications by plant, department and shift, which shall be open to the inspection of the Shop Committee at all reasonable times, a copy of which shall be given to the Chief Steward at least quarterly.

SEC. 3. Employees shall acquire seniority after ninety (90) days from date of hiring, after the expiration of which period their seniority shall be as of the date of hiring. The employment of any such probationary employee may be terminated by the Company for any reason except that such probationary employee shall not be discharged for engaging in lawful union activities. If any such probationary employee is laid off, he/she shall have a right to recall on the regular seniority basis, and if recalled, will continue on the unexpired portion of the ninety (90) day probationary period.

SEC. 4. Employees shall lose their seniority if:

(a) They quit.

(b) They are discharged for cause.

(c) They are absent from work three (3) consecutive working days without notifying the shift superintendent or supervisor, unless they have reasonable excuse why such notification was not made.

(d) They fail to report the first day following the expiration on an approved leave of absence, unless a satisfactory reason for such failure is given.

(e) They make any false statements in obtaining or renewing a leave of absence.

(f) They work elsewhere during a leave of absence.

(g) They retire.

(h) They fail to report to work within three (3) working days or at the beginning of the shift on the 4th day after they are notified by registered mail, return receipt requested, to return to work, provided that employees shall not be deprived of seniority, if their failure to return to work is caused by sickness or injury, or for reason beyond their control, and notice thereof is given the Company at the earliest practical time. If requested by employees, the Company and the shop committee shall determine the justice of the claim that employees had good reason to fail to report for work when called.

(i) They are laid off for twelve (12) consecutive months. However, if their seniority exceeds twelve (12) months, they shall not lose their seniority until they are laid off for a continuous period equal to their seniority. However, employees with five or more years' seniority shall break seniority if they are laid off in excess of five continuous years.

SEC. 5. Seniority shall start from the last date of hiring except that employees who have been laid off through no fault of their own and have been recalled within the time allowed by Paragraph (i) of Section 4 of this Article, shall retain their seniority from their original date of hiring.

SEC. 6. Seniority shall entitle an employee to preference over employees with later hiring dates, in case of layoff or recall to work subject to the provisions of this Agreement. When there is a decrease in force, the following procedure shall be followed:

(a) All employees having no seniority shall be laid off first.

(b) When it becomes necessary to further reduce the number of employees in any department the lowest employees on the seniority list will be laid off and any other employees affected shall be transferred on the basis of seniority to any other department where there is an opening created by the layoff. Among the employees being transferred, ability, merit and capacity being equal, the employee with the most seniority shall receive the preference of the jobs available.

(c) Employees transferred as a result of layoff or recall procedure shall receive the rate for the department in which they are working which bears the same relation to maximum rate as they were receiving before transfer.

(d) When there is a decrease in force in any department, the remaining employees must accept shift and plant assignments according to their respective seniority.

SEC. 7. In the event the Company feels that strict application of seniority during a layoff affects a plant operation or operations, it can ask that the Company and the Union negotiate changes in order of strict seniority in order to avoid undue hardship.

SEC. 8. In the event of increasing the force in any department after a reduction in force, employees who were transferred as a result of layoff and are still working in the plant, will be transferred back on the basis of their departmental listing. When there is an increase in force, employees laid off shall be recalled to work within the plant in the order of their plant-wide seniority provided they are able to perform a job which is open.

SEC. 9. At least two working days' notice will be given to the shop committee and the employee before a layoff. On recalls employees shall be given three (3) working days' notice by registered mail, return receipt requested, in which to report for work.

SEC. 10. The transferring of employees is the sole responsibility of management, subject to the following:

Job vacancies and newly created jobs will be filled as follows:

(a) A job vacancy or newly created job will be posted on the bulletin board for two working days.

(b) Employees who make written application on forms provided by the Company will be given preference in filling such openings. Selections shall be based primarily on ability to do the job but when all qualifications are equal, the employee with most seniority shall receive the preference.

(c) Any secondary job opening resulting from filling posted jobs will be filled without posting through promotion, transfer, or by new hire, but ability, merit and capacity being equal, the senior employee will be given first consideration by the Company.

(d) An employee who bids on and accepts a posted job shall not be eligible to bid on another job for twelve (12) months, except in cases of an involuntary transfer.

SEC. 11.

(a) Preference of plant and shift will be given to seniority employees once a year within their department. Should an employee elect to exercise such preference, he shall not again exercise such preference for the next twelve (12) months unless involuntarily transferred in which case he may again exercise preference.

(b) It is recognized that the needs of the business require a division of skills on each shift and between plants and that this division of skills shall continue to exist in the future as it has in the past. If the needs of the business or personal emergencies require temporary modification (not exceeding 30 days) in the last choice of shift or plant, a modification shall be agreed upon by management and the shop committee.

SEC. 12. Employees shall not be transferred on a temporary basis to another department when regular employees have been told to stay home from that department (except for the purpose of equalization of hours).

SEC. 13. Any employee transferred from a job in the bargaining unit to any position excluded therefrom in Article I, Section 1, of this Agreement, shall be credited with the actual seniority he/she would be entitled to under the Agreement and shall be reinstated as a member of the Union in the event he/ she at any time is returned to the bargaining unit for any reason; employees hired in on any excluded job shall not have seniority.

SEC. 14. Employees handicapped by major physical disabilities due to injury received on the job may be made exempt by the Company and Union from the operations of these seniority provisions in the event of layoff.

SEC. 15. Any deviation from the seniority provisions of this contract shall be by mutual agreement between the Company and the shop committee.

SEC. 16. The members of the shop committee shall head the seniority list in the plant and shall be the last persons to be laid off and the first to be recalled. They shall be returned to their original standing on the seniority list upon termination of service on such committee. Stewards shall be the last to be laid off and the first to be recalled among the shift or group by whom they are elected and whom they represent. Members of the shop committee and Stewards shall be assigned and shall have the right to make transfers in accordance with their natural seniority, provided however, that the shop committeeperson and the Steward shall not be temporarily transferred out of their department as long as there is work in the department on the shift other than leaders' work. A Steward or committeeperson shall have the right to work on any Sunday on which work is scheduled on his shift or in his area of jurisdiction, provided he can perform one of the jobs available.

ARTICLE VII
LEAVES OF ABSENCE

SEC. 1. Leave of absence for personal reasons for not more than 60 days may be granted upon written application filed with the Company and the Chief Steward and approval of the Company and the Union. Such leave of absence may be renewed for good cause for periods not in excess of 60-day periods. Seniority shall accumulate. Any employee misrepresenting his/her reason for request for leave of absence or who engages in other employment shall be subject to discharge.

SEC. 2. Any employee elected to a permanent office of the Union or as a delegate to any labor activity necessitating a temporary leave of absence, shall be granted such leave of absence and shall at the end of the term in the first instance or at the end of the mission in the second instance be guaranteed reemployment with accumulated seniority if there is sufficient work for which he/she is in line at the then current rate of pay.

SEC. 3. During temporary leaves of absence, the employee's job shall not be considered vacant and shall be filed by the Company on a temporary basis. Personal leaves of absence shall be considered temporary for this purpose.

ARTICLE VIII
HOURS AND OVERTIME RATES

SEC. 1. The regular work week shall commence at 7:00 A.M. Monday morning and end the following Monday morning at 7:00 A.M. The regular schedule of hours shall be eight (8) hours in one day and forty (40) hours a week at straight time pay.

SEC. 2. Time and one-half shall be paid for the first two hours overtime after eight (8) hours straight time in any one day, Monday through Friday inclusive, and for all time worked over forty (40) hours in any one work week and the first eight (8) hours on a Saturday.

SEC. 3. Double time shall be paid for all work performed on a Sunday and on the following designated holidays: New Year's Day, Martin Luther King, Jr. Day, Presidents' Day, Memorial Day, Fourth of July, Labor Day, Thanksgiving Day, Friday after Thanksgiving Day, Christmas Day and all hours in excess of four (4) on Christmas Eve and New Year's Eve or the alternate day if one is designated under Article IX, Section 8, and over ten (10) hours in any one day, Monday through Friday and over eight (8) hours on Saturday.

SEC. 4. The Company will divide both regular work and overtime work as equitably as possible. For this purpose, separate records will be kept for each department on each shift at each plant. Division of regular work hours when all departments are scheduled to work shall be on a plant-wide and shift-wide basis. Division of overtime hours, when only part of the departments are scheduled to work, shall be on a departmental basis, in each plant on each shift. The Company will attempt to equalize hours between shifts, that is, where it is possible to assign work to the shift where hours are lowest without disturbing production sequences, the work shall be so assigned. Drivers shall divide all hours as a separate unit, by plants. Maintenance employees performing skilled maintenance work shall divide all hours as one unit for both plants. There shall not be more than 32 hours differential on such equalization lists, which shall be kept for each four month period, provided that on the plant-wide list, the low man is able to do work available to equalize the time.

SEC. 5. If employees report for work on their regular shift and are sent home because there is no work available, they shall receive two hours' pay provided they had received no notice not to report, and provided they have not refused to do any work offered them. Employees who commence work shall be paid for a minimum of four hours' work provided they have not refused to do any work offered them.

Employees who are called in for work outside of regular shift or on a Sunday or legal holiday shall be paid for a minimum of four hours' work.

SEC. 6. In no case shall overtime be compulsory. In the event however, an employee agrees to and is scheduled to work overtime and does not notify the Company in advance that he will not report and then is absent unless for reasons beyond his control it shall be considered absenteeism the same as failure to report on a regular work day.

SEC. 7. The allowance of an overtime premium on any hour excludes that hour from consideration for overtime on any other basis, thus eliminating any double overtime payments.

SEC. 8. The Company will continue the established practice of affording a 25-minute paid lunch period during each 8-hour shift. The employees will not ring their time cards "out" and "in" as the 25 minutes are part of the regular schedule of 8 hours a day and 40 hours a week for which they are paid at the regular straight time rate.

ARTICLE IX
WAGES

SEC. 1. Wage rates for all departments shall be those stated in the wage schedule attached hereto, marked Exhibit A. Such wage rates include a general wage increase of 3 per hour effective as of March 1, 2011, and also the amount of 1 per hour transferred from cost-of-living allowance which heretofore has been 2 per hour and shall now become 1 per hour, subject to adjustment in accordance with Section 12 of this Article. A general wage increase for all employees shall become effective March 1, 2013, as also stated in the wage schedule attached hereto, marked Exhibit A.

SEC. 2. Shift premium will be paid in addition to regular pay as follows:

Afternoon Shift	$0.50 per hour
Midnight Shift	$1.00 per hour

Afternoon shift normally begins at 3:00 P.M. Midnight shift at 11:00. P.M. An employee working other than normal shifts shall receive the shift premium, if any, of the shift in which four (4) or more hours fall. Employees working four (4) or more hours of overtime into another shift shall receive the shift premiums of the shift for all such overtime hours.

SEC. 3. Bonus. The fact that the Company has from time to time in the past paid bonuses to its employees shall not in any way be considered as precedent for the payment of any bonus in the future by the Company, but this provision shall not preclude the Company from paying any bonus.

SEC. 4. Current Profit Sharing Plan. All production over 10% of profit on sales per month will be divided with the hourly rated employees on a 50-50 basis as follows:

(a) 50% retained by the Company and 50% paid to the hourly rate employees in the ratio that the total number of hours worked during each month, including overtime, for each employee bears to the total of such hours for all employees. (This means that all hourly rate employees will receive the same hourly rate of payment).

(b) Payment of this sum, if any, will be paid as soon after the first of each month as the computation can be made by the Controller of the Company.

(c) It is the intent of this plan to retain for the Company a minimum of 10% profit on sales on an annual basis because this is the minimum on which the Company can successfully operate; therefore, if in any month profits become less than 10%, this amount will be made up in succeeding months before distribution to employees.

SEC. 5. Insurance.

(a) The Company will continue its present group insurance plan for all employees to provide the following types of insurance:

Life insurance 20,000.00

Accidental Death and Dismemberment
Insurance 20,000.00

Accident and Sickness Weekly Benefits for 26 weeks
during any illness 150.00

Hospital benefit for employees and dependents — full coverage for all hospital charges for semi-private room up to 120 days for any one continuous period of hospital service.

Surgical benefits . . . . Up to 10,000.00

The cost of such insurance shall be paid partly by the Company and partly by the employees on the same basis as has been in effect heretofore, until March 1, 2000.

(b) Until March 1, 2013, a fund of money will be provided to be used to pay $50.00 a week to employees who are drawing Worker's Compensation or weekly indemnity under our sick and accident insurance plan. This $50.00 will supplement such benefits and be paid directly by the Company out of the fund which will be provided as follows: "As near as possible, the Company will keep a fund of approximately $50,000.00 to pay these benefits. If possible, the $50,000.00 will be set aside during months when the Company is making more than 10% profit on sales. If at any time the Company is not making the 10% profit and the fund has diminished so that the benefits cannot be paid and there is need to replenish the fund, then a payroll deduction of $2.50 a month will be made and a like contribution made by the Company to replenish the fund up to $50,000.00. The fund will be kept intact in this way so that all employees will get the $50.00 a week whenever they are disabled and drawing either Worker's Compensation or disability indemnity including the first week for a compensable accident. "

(c) Commencing March 1, 2000, the Company will pay the entire cost of the following insurance coverage:

Life insurance $25,000.00

Accidental Death and Dismemberment Insurance . .   25,000.00

Accident and Sickness Weekly Benefits for 26 weeks
during any illness, first day accident, eighth day
sickness, plus Workers' Compensation Supplement . .   160.00

Hospital benefits for employees and dependents for semi-private room up to 120 days for any one continuous period of hospital service.

Surgical benefits . . . .   Up to 10,000.00

SEC. 6. Deferred Profit Sharing Plan. The Company will continue its Deferred Profit Sharing Plan established in 1942, for the benefit of the employees, as amended. For the complete provisions, reference is made to the agreement. The following is a synopsis.

The objects of the Plan are to assist the employees in accumulating a saving for use in later years and to share the profits of the Company. All employees participate in the benefits of the plan starting the first of the month following the acquiring of seniority. The Plan provided for a contribution of the Trust of 20% of the annual profits of the Company before provision for Federal Income Tax as determined by an independent Certified Public Accountant. (Also see Sec. 13 of this Article). The Trustee invests funds in such investments as are legal investments for trustees under the laws of this State. A separate account is kept by the Trustee for each participant and to which the participant's share is credited. The annual share of each participant is equal to a percentage of his total annual compensation. The same percentage is applied to every employee each year but varies from year to year, according to the amount of profit made by the Company.

Benefits are paid by the Trustees to the participants in the following five situations:

(a) After ten years' participation at 10% per year upon application showing financial necessity.

(b) Permanent total disability — (one lump sum).

(c) Death — (one lump sum to designated beneficiary).

(d) Retirement — (lump sum, in equal payments spread over 5 years, or an annuity).

(e) Severance of Employment — (See Sec. 13 of this Article).

SEC. 7. Free Gloves. The Company will furnish gloves free to each employee on this basis — every employee needing gloves on his job will be furnished a pair. If new gloves are needed, he/she must turn in his/her old gloves. If he/she loses his/her gloves, he/she will have to pay for a replacement at the cost to the Company.

SEC. 8. Paid Holidays. Each employee who has been on the payroll thirty (30) or more calendar days before New Year's Day, Martin Luther King, Jr. Day, Presidents' Day, Memorial Day, Fourth of July, Thanksgiving Day, Friday after

Thanksgiving Day, Labor Day and Christmas Day shall be paid eight (8) hours at his/her straight time rate providing he/she has worked all hours offered him/her during the week in which the holiday occurs or has a just reason for any absence which has been approved by management and the shop committee. This provision for paid holidays is in addition to the provision for double time on these specified holidays which is provided for in Section 3 of Article VIII of this contract. All employees shall receive four (4) hours pay without work at their regular straight time rate on Christmas Eve and New Year's Eve, provided, however, that for employees who agree to work such hours on Christmas Eve or New Year's Eve, the Company may designate an alternate day or days to be agreed upon with employee on which such employees shall be entitled to receive four hours pay without work, and double time under Section 3 of Article VIII if they work.

SEC. 9. Merit Increases will be granted when approved by a majority of the following five (5) individuals: Shift committeeperson, shift steward, shift leader, shift superintendent and assistant shift superintendent, in accordance with the following schedule:

(a) New employees. New employees will be considered for merit increases beginning the first pay period after the acquisition of 6 months' seniority, 12 months' seniority, etc., after each six (6) months' additional seniority until the employee has reached the maximum of his classification.

(b) Present employees. All present employees will be eligible for consideration for merit increases in the same manner as above prescribed for new employees at the time they have acquired 6 months' seniority, 12 months' seniority, etc.

(c) Veterans. Upon the return to service at the Company, by veterans, special consideration for merit increases shall be granted so that as the veterans warrant merit increases in the opinion of the Merit Review Committee, there shall be merit increases granted in the amount which will bring them to the rate they would have received had they not been in service. It is understood that these increases shall be merit increases and not length of service increases and shall be granted only on the basis of merit. The purpose of this supplement is to permit merit increases of more than $.05 an hour each six (6) months.

SEC. 10. Time off for funeral. Each employee shall be entitled to three days off to attend a funeral for a member of his/her immediate family, which shall be construed to be his/her spouse, children, parents, grandparents of the employee, parents-in-law, brothers and sisters, and shall be paid for three eight-hour days at his/her regular straight time pay.

SEC. 11. Employees sustaining injuries in the plant requiring medical attention will be permitted to leave the plant during working hours on the day of the injury to secure medical attention and will be compensated for necessary time lost during their regular schedule of work on that day. In the event that the injury is such that the attending physician advises the employee not to return to work, he/she will be compensated only for the balance of his/her scheduled day. In the event the injury is such that the employee is permitted to work, but is required by the physician to make additional visits for necessary medical attention, and if such visits are to be made during the employee's shift hours, the same rule will apply with respect to such recurrent visits.

SEC. 12. All employees covered by this Agreement shall be paid a cost-of-living allowance at the times and in accordance with the formula set forth in the 1988 Collective Bargaining Agreement Between General Motors Corporation and UAW.

SEC. 13. GAW — The Company agrees to continue the provision in its present Trust to improve the security provided on layoffs as follows:

(a) Employees shall participate as soon as they acquire seniority.

(b) The Company shall contribute out of profits an amount equal to $.10 for each straight time hour worked by each employee with less than three years' seniority, in addition to 20% of profits. This $.10 per straight time hour additional contribution will be set aside each month and will be owned by each employee as his/her own layoff fund, in addition to the Company contribution, earnings, etc. It will be available not only on layoff, but in accordance with the terms of the Trust — retirement, death, disability and similar benefits.

(c) The formula for pay out on layoff provides that upon severance of employment by layoff, the fund will be paid weekly in an amount equal to the difference between his/her unemployment compensation and 65% of his/her net take-home pay.

(d) This proposal creates a fund for each employee during the first three years at the Company of $.10 per hour, plus the allocated share of the Company's contribution which will be available in the event of a layoff, as well as the other contingencies provided in the Trust.

(e) When an employee acquires three years' seniority and the preferred allocation to his Trust of $.10 per hour terminates, the $.10 per hour will be included in his/her individual rate.

SEC. 14. In addition to the provision for retirement in Article XII, Section 3, of our Deferred Profit Sharing Trust, the Company agrees to pay a retired employee $100.00 a month for two years and also to provide Retiree's Insurance for life in accordance with the following schedule:

Years of Credited Service in Retirement Plan at Retirement	Amount of Continuing Group Life Insurance
30 or more	$20,000.00
20 but less than 30	$15,000.00
10 but less than 20	$10,000.00
Less than 10	None

Retired employees shall not make any contribution towards the cost of this coverage. An employee must file an application for normal retirement under the Retirement Plan in order to be covered by this insurance, whether or not he/ she is eligible for a retirement benefit from the Retirement Trust.

SEC. 15. Leaders. The Company shall determine the need for a leader or leaders in each department. Leader vacancies and leader openings shall be posted plant-wide and shall be filled in accordance with Section 10(b) of Article VI. It shall be the policy of the Company to appoint a leader for any group of three (3) or more workers. Leaders shall equalize their hours in the same manner as all other employees. All permanent leaders shall receive 5 over the job rate they are leading. The Company may request an employee to accept a leader job on a temporary basis. If the employee accepts such temporary assignment he/she shall be paid from 3 to 5 above job rate for all days in which he/she spends the majority of his/her hours as a leader.

Duties of leaders in addition to their regular work assignments shall include:

(a) Instructing employees in the group they lead.

(b) Assisting in correcting difficulties encountered by employees in their group.

(c) Distributing job or making work assignments under supervision of the supervisor or superintendent.

(d) Leaders shall not pass opinions concerning other employees to management concerning disciplinary action, hire, discharge, or discipline an employee or assume any other supervisory responsibility of management.

ARTICLE X
GENERAL

SEC. 1. A union bulletin board shall be provided near the time clock which may be used for any purpose desired by the Union Committee. The Company shall not be considered as having approved the contents of the notices posted by the Union.

SEC. 2. The Union agrees that its members will not carry on Union activities in the plant or on the premises of the Company during working hours. The lunch period shall not be considered working hours.

SEC. 3. This Agreement and the Supplemental Unemployment Benefit Agreement dated this 4th day of May, 2011, constitute the entire Agreement between the Union and the Company, and all other agreements oral or written except those listed in Exhibit A and Exhibit B attached hereto are hereby cancelled.

SEC. 4. Work normally done by skilled maintenance employees during regular work hours will be done by maintenance employees on overtime. During such time, as well as on regular shifts when maintenance workers are not assigned, production employees may perform such minor jobs as changing recorder batteries, installing temporary pump in nitriding, changing thermocouples, etc.

SEC. 5. Definitions.

"Working Days" as used in this Contract means Monday through Friday.

The word "transfer" means the assignment of an employee from one department to another, one shift to another or from one plant to another.

The word "layoff" means a separation of employment due to reduction of force. Under these circumstances the laid-off employee retains a right to be recalled for reemployment under the seniority provisions of our Contract. The laid-off employee also has a right to continuation of insurance as provided in our Contract.

Except for Maintenance, the word "department" means both the physical area designated as a department by the Company and the classification of the employees working in that area.

SEC. 6. There shall be a shop safety committee in each plant consisting of three (3) members designated by the Union and three (3) members designated by the Company which shall establish shop safety practices and conditions. The committee shall meet monthly and report to the Company and the shop committee. The recommendations of the committee shall be placed in effect by the Company as soon as practical. The committee shall adopt shop safety rules. Any employee failing to conform to such rules shall be subject to disciplinary action.

ARTICLE XI
TERMINATION

SEC. 1. This Agreement shall become effective upon its acceptance by the Union and the Company and shall remain in force through March 31, 2014, and thereafter for successive periods of one year unless either party shall on or before November 1st serve written notice on the other party of a desire to terminate or amend this Agreement. A notice of desire to amend shall have the effect of terminating the entire Agreement at 12:01 A.M. on March 31, 2014, or at 12:01 A.M. of March 31st of any later year in the same manner as a notice of desire to terminate, unless before March 31, 2014 (or any subsequent year) all subjects of amendment proposed by either party have been disposed of by agreement or by withdrawal by the party proposing the amendment. IN WITNESS WHEREOF the parties hereto have set their hands and seals this 4th day of May, 2011.

EXHIBIT "A"

It is understood that the hiring-in rate shown opposite the respective department is for inexperienced help. Experienced help shall have a starting rate commensurate with their previous experience and ability.

The hiring-in rate is for day workers only. Afternoon shift employees will receive a $0.50 premium and Midnight shift employees will receive a $1.00 premium in addition to rates shown. Merit increases from the hiring-in rate shall be $0.25 each six (6) months in accordance with the merit increase provisions of this Contract. The last $0.25 of merit spread shall not be granted to any employee until he has accumulated three (3) years' seniority.

HOURLY WAGE RATES
Effective March 1, 2011

Department	Hire	Top Rate	Leaders
Aircraft	14.44	16.28	16.78
Atmosphere	14.34	16.18	16.68
Blast & Clean	14.24	16.08	16.58
Bright Hardening	14.34	16.18	16.68
Carburize	14.34	16.18	16.68
Drivers	14.24	16.08	16.58
Heat Treat	14.34	16.18	16.68
High Speed	14.44	16.28	16.78
Inspect	14.34	16.18	16.78
Receiving & Shipping	14.24	16.08	16.58
Salt Bath	14.34	16.18	16.68
Straightening	14.44	16.28	16.78
Tool Steel	14.44	16.28	16.78
Maintenance			
Shift Leaders	15.60	17.40	
General Maintenance	15.40	16.20	
Carpenters	15.02	17.80	
Plumbers	15.20	17.04	
Welders	15.20	17.04	
Electricians	15.20	17.04	
Temp. Control & Instrm. Rep			
. . . .	15.20	17.04	
Machine Repair	15.20	17.04	
Painters	15.12	16.90	
Furnace Repair	15.02	16.80	
Maintenance Helpers	14.44	15.70	
Employees in Training	14.44	15.80	
Janitors	14.34	15.50	

*Effective March 1, 2013

Department	Hire	Top Rate	Leaders
Aircraft	14.98	16.98	17.48
Atmosphere	14.88	16.88	17.38
Blast & Clean	14.78	16.78	17.28
Bright Hardening	14.88	16.88	17.38
Carburize	14.88	16.88	17.38
Drivers	14.78	16.78	17.28
Heat Treat	14.88	16.88	17.38
High Speed	14.88	16.88	17.38
Inspect	14.88	16.88	17.38
Receiving & Shipping	14.78	16.78	17.28
Salt Bath	14.88	16.88	17.38
Straightening	14.98	16.98	17.48

Department	Hire	Top Rate	Leaders
Tool Steel	14.98	16.98	17.48

Department	Hire	Top Rate
Maintenance		
Shift Leaders	16.26	18.24
General Maintenance	16.06	18.04
Carpenters	15.68	17.66
Plumbers	15.86	17.84
Welders	15.86	17.84
Electricians	15.86	17.84
Temp. Control & Instrm.		
Rep.	15.86	17.84
Machine Repair	15.86	17.84
Painters	15.78	17.76
Furnace Repair	15.68	17.66
Maintenance Helpers	14.98	16.56
Employees in Training	14.98	16.56
Janitors	14.88	16.46

EXHIBIT "B"
Vacations

SEC. 1. Every employee who has been in the employ of the Company for six (6) months or more on any 1st of any year shall be entitled to a vacation in accordance with the following schedule:

Length of Service	Time Off	Pay
6 months but less than 1 year	1 week	22 hours
1 year but less than 2 years	1 week	44 hours
2 years but less than 5 years	2 weeks	88 hours
5 years but less than 20 years	3 weeks	132 hours
20 years or more.	4 weeks	176 hours

SEC. 2. The vacation pay for the hours indicated above shall be computed at the employee's straight time hourly rate.

SEC. 3. It is agreed that May 1st of each year shall be the date for determining the length of time an employee has worked and the amount of vacation pay each employee shall be entitled to. Any employee who voluntarily quits or who is discharged prior to May 1st of each year shall not be entitled to any vacation with pay or vacation pay allowance for that year.

SEC. 4. The purpose of vacations being to provide rest and recreation, it is agreed that all employees shall take time off as a vacation for at least as long as the schedule provides.

SEC. 5. Vacations must be taken between May 1st and October 31st of the vacation year. Time off must be taken during a full payroll week and there shall be no split payroll weeks for any scheduled vacation. The vacation schedule and any exceptions to this vacation plan will be made by the Shift Superintendent and the Shift Committeepersons.

SEC. 6. If an employee has been laid off during the vacation year and has been recalled to work on or before the following October 31st, he/she shall be eligible to receive full vacation pay if he/she has worked 26 weeks or more during the vacation year. If he/she has worked less than 26 weeks, he/she shall receive a fractional vacation pay equal to the number of weeks worked during the vacation year over 52. For example, if a recalled employee has worked 14 weeks on May 1st, he/she would get 14/52 vacation allowance.

SEC. 7. Vacation pay shall be paid on the regular pay day of the vacation period of each employee.